Your eBook Survival Kit

Dr David P Reiter

16

EasyRead Large

RHYW

Copyright Page from the Original Book

Digital Publishing Centre
an imprint of IP (Interactive Publications Pty Ltd)
Treetop Studio, 9 Kuhler Court
Carindale, Queensland, Australia 4152
sales@ipoz.biz
ipoz.biz/IP/IP.htm

First published by IP in 2011

National Library of Australia

Cataloguing-in-Publication entry:

Author: Reiter, David P. (David Philip)

Title: Your ebook survival kit [electronic resource] / David P Reiter. 2nd edition

ISBN: 9781921479960 (eBk)

Subjects: Electronic publications--Handbooks, manuals, etc.
Electronic publishing--Handbooks, manuals, etc.

TABLE OF CONTENTS

Author's Note

This kit should be treated as a guide, rather than a Bible. It's based on practical experience I and my staff at

IP have gained preparing books for eBook publication through our Digital Publishing Centre.

IP is a market leader in digital publishing in Australia. An independent publisher, we have gained this expertise from our own efforts and resources, which should make the lessons in the Kit very relevant to small publishers and individuals wanting to learn just enough to publish and market eBooks effectively.

You may not want to produce eBook files yourself but rather get to the point where you better understand the process of moving from print to digital. This will help you learn what's possible in the digital environment and how best to prepare files at the print stage to minimize the effort required to convert them to eBook formats.

The Kit itself began as a serial, with subscribers receiving an issue per week from the first edition over three to four months. Subscribers could ask questions and provide feedback at any stage, and in my revisions I took that feedback into account – as well as updating the content to reflect the constantly changing digital environment.

The Kit is not intended to be exhaustive in its coverage of software for preparing files for eBook publication. The aim is to give you an efficient and user-friendly methodology to produce eBook files that will work across as many platforms as possible – without you needing a degree in IT to get there. Hardware and software evolve, sometimes faster than we might like, but this Kit will make you aware of strategies and workflows that will hold you in good stead for the foreseeable future, i.e. the end of this year!

The Kit is being published exclusively as an eBook for several reasons, but the most important is to make it easy to update as necessary. Updates will be posted to the Digital Publishing Centre's Facebook and Twitter sites, and we may well issue a revised edition yearly, depending on feedback from our social networking sites. We encourage you to follow us online and join the chat about things digital.

I'd like to acknowledge the feedback from subscribers to the Kit, who asked questions throughout the two months when the issues were being circulated. And I'd like to thank Anna McGuire for her helpful suggestions and Candice Poole, Lauren Daniels and TJ Withers for their valuable editorial assistance.

–David P Reiter

Key Terms

Adobe Creative Suite: a software package containing key programs used to prepare print and digital files, such as InDesign, Photoshop, Flash, Distiller and Acrobat.

.aif or .aiff: Audio Interchange File Format for storing audio at stereo quality. Audio .aiff files can be compressed into mp3 or mp4 for eBook publication.

Anchor: the specific place you get to when you click on a link in a file.

Calibre: a free emulator that allows you to view your digital file on a variety of virtual Readers and also upload files from your computer to your Reader. It can also be used to convert between certain formats, e.g. mobi to ePub and vice versa.

Character Styles: consistent coding attached to a character, word or phrases, defining its characteristics within a paragraph, e.g. italics.

Conversion: the process by which a word processed or print ready ("press-ready") file is prepared for eBook publication, generally via eBook editing software. Sites such as Amazon and Smashwords provide online converters for producing files that will work in the main eBook formats.

Digital Publishing Centre: IP's section that specialises in the preparation of files for print on demand (POD) or eBook publication.

Dreamweaver: the html editor from Adobe (see a dobe.com) that you can use to refine xhtml output (from a file exported from InDesign) before uploading to Amazon for the Kindle Reader.

eBook: a digital file that may contain text, visual, and audio content.

eBook Reader or Reader or eReader: hardware that can download or import digital files and view or play their content.

Emulator: a software program such as Calibre or Adobe Digital Editions (ADE) that allows you to preview how files will display on particular Readers.

ePub: developed and refined by The International Digital Publishing Forum, ePub is a key cross-platform format for containing compressed eBook content.

epubcheck: free application for checking the correctness of coding within an ePub file before it is uploaded for publication.

Flash (.swf): content created in Adobe (see adob e.com), generally with audio, video and animated features. Flash content will play on Readers compatible with Adobe's Flash Player. Note: the iPad and iPhone are not compatible with Flash at this time.

Font: typefaces for displaying text. When fonts are properly defined by character and paragraph styles before conversion, they are more likely to display similar to the print original.

Google Android: an operating system expected to be a main competitor for the iPad/iPhone in the Windows environment. Google also maintains an eBook store from which they sell generic ePub and pdf files.

Hyperlinks or links: coding that references a starting point with its destination. When users click on a link they are taken to the destination defined by the link.

InDesign: a key software component from Adobe (see adobe.com) that is used to prepare press-ready pdfs for printing and optimized pdfs for digital distribution, and more recently, for preliminary formatting of xhtml and ePub files.

Interactivity: encouraging reader involvement with the title by means of internal or external links, or choices to play multimedia enhancements such as audio or video that are contained within the file. Some Readers come with social networking connectivity, so that you can chat with your friends while reading a file.

iPad: Apple's maxi Reader, offering a full colour display and many of the advanced features of a laptop or notebook computer. Users may download directly onto their iPad from the iBookstore, or from online stores offering ePub or pdf files. It is also possible to sync (synchronise) downloaded files from a computer onto an iPad or iPhone. The latest version at this time is the iPad 4 (November 2012), which boasts a Retina Display that provides high resolution visibility of content.

ISBN: the International Serial Book Number that is a unique identifier for each version of a publication. Critical for preparing metadata to go with the eBook file.

iBook Author: a free application from Apple (see apple.com) that can produce proprietary files designed for viewing on iOS devices such as *iPads* and *iPhones.*

iTunes/iTunes Store: first port of call for music, eBooks and apps via the free iTunes software marketed by Apple (see apple.com). Also provides *iTunes Connect,* a portal for publishers uploading content to the *iBookstore.*

Kindle Reader: a family of reading devices, including "eInk" grayscale viewers, as well as colour devices such as the *Kindle Fire,* produced by Amazon (see a mazon.com). Titles are produced in proprietary KF8 or .mobi formats and are tested offline via *Kindle Previewer* program. Users must purchase and download files from Amazon via their Whisperlite network for display on their Kindle or by means of emulating software such as Kindle for PC or Kindle for Mac (a.k.a. the Kindle App).

Kobo Reader: a device associated with Borders/Chapters/Indigo. eBook content can be downloaded from the Kobo Store.

LTE (Long-term Evolution): is a specialised form of telephony (electronic transmission) in the 4G broadcasting system.

mp3/mp4: compressed audio files, offering near stereo quality, playable on most smartphones and Readers. Also known as AAC files.

Nook: a family of reading devices produced by Barnes & Noble, an American physical and digital book chainstore.

Paragraph Styles: consistent coding attached to a paragraph, defining its font, margins, justification, margins and spaces before and after.

pdf: the portable document format, primarily associated with Adobe (see adobe.com), providing the ability to produce files that will appear the same across a variety of reading devices. pdfs can contain multimedia elements like video and audio, and can provide interactivity via links to content within the file or to external content on websites.

Photoshop: the image creation, editing and optimizing software from Adobe (see adobe.com).

POD/Print on Demand: a digital process for producing physical books from a digital master at a stable unit cost.

Point or pt: unit of measurement within a digital file. The relative size may vary depending on the font used.

postscript: a means of capturing, marking up and embedding digital content so that it will display the same across platforms. InDesign files output as postscript (.ps) files before creating a pdf master via Adobe Distiller.

Pre-publication: all the tasks associated with preparing a file for publication, including the preparation of a master file.

Packagers or Book Packagers: companies that take your word processed file and prepare it for print and/or digital publication.

Quicktime: a cross-platform software package capable of displaying audio/video content via Quicktime Platform, a free download from apple.com.

rich text format (.rtf): files that can contain text and visuals prior to conversion into eBook formats, in either the WIndows or Mac operating systems.

Sigil: a free cross-platform software package for editing and refining ePub files.

Sony Reader: a Reader marketed by Sony, which can access eBook content from the Sony Store.

Specs/specifications: rules for preparing eBook files before uploading them to specific eBook distributors.

Territories: the world used to be divided into geographical areas where publishers could license rights to sell a title. The licence can be as limited as a single country or as broad as the globe. So a book can potentially have many publishers exercizing rights in a particular territory, or a single one holding world rights. IP routinely holds world rights for its titles.

3G/4G: networks that send and receive digital content online via smartphones or Readers. Users either have to pay an access fee or purchase a Reader with free 3G/4G capability to access online content.

.wav or Waveform Audio File Format: stores compressed audio for presentation on the Windows Media Player.

Wi-Fi: a microwave network that sends or receives content via 'hot spots'. Most current eBook reading devices have inbuilt wi-fi capabilities.

xhtml: similar to html, or web mark-up language, but these files are 'zipped' to contain content for transmission.

xml or Extensible Markup Language: allows publishers to 'future-proof' their titles by applying coding conventions that work across multiple platforms before converting files into final eBook formats.

eMyths and eRealities

What follows in this section is Big Picture stuff – an overview of the issues to be discussed in greater detail in the body of the Kit.

Let's deal with ten key myths first:

1. An eBook is an eBook is an eBook

It isn't. eBooks come in all shapes and sizes. An eBook can comprise text on its own, or it can include images, sound, animation and even interactivity. What you can do with your eBook is limited only by your imagination. Or, if you plan to publish yourself, what you can do is limited by your technical expertise.

2. One eBook Reader is much the same as another

Some are, some aren't. Readers (i.e. eBook reading devices) come in all shapes and sizes. The Kindle and iPad and a few others are relatively BIG. Smartphones like the iPhone are small. More and more Readers, as I'll refer to them from now on, are springing up to give consumers more choices. This makes the production and delivery of content more challenging for publishers. Some tablets like the iPad are getting smaller to meet competitors like Amazon's Kindle and Barnes & Noble's Nook, while some smartphones are getting bigger and are referred to by some people as "phablets".

Readers have varying amounts of space on their screens for displaying your content. Some can display landscape (wide) as well as in portrait (tall) format, essentially rolling with the content. So, if you like to create wide content like two page spreads, you may have problems displaying it on a Reader designed for portrait content. Or, it may display but the content may be unreadable except for those with magnifying glasses.

Most Readers can display colour, while older and cheaper models only display black and white.

Some are excellent at displaying images, others aren't much better at that than a fax machine.

Some can play audio and even movies, or connect to the internet, while others do only static stuff and only connect to the internet to take your money when you buy a book.

3. Once you create a pdf, you have an eBook

What's a pdf? How much time do you have to talk through this? Put simply, it's a cross-platform file format that lets your reader see your work just as you see it before it's published. In other words, what you see is what they get.

It would be nice if all eBook Readers accepted eBooks for publication in pdf format, but they don't.

In fact fewer do than don't. And even those that do may require you to send them a special kind of pdf for their Reader.

Truth is, there are almost as many kinds of formats for reading devices as there are Readers. This is because certain companies – not mentioning any names – want to keep you hooked on their Readers by ensuring that the books you buy only work on *their* Reader.

This means if you want your book to work on ALL Readers, you'll have to find a way to send the distributors your content in a file format that will work on each Reader. Or you'll have to publish the same work in different formats suited to the major Readers.

Given that Amazon make about two-thirds of all eBook sales at present, I would certainly start with a .mobi file and branch out from there as your budget and/or patience allows.

And you thought it was going to be easy? Or at least not this complicated!

4. Is Conversion is a religious experience?

You may find yourself invoking God's name more than once while creating your eBook, but the *conversion* process has little to do with having your head dipped into water.

It means starting with an original *master file* and converting this into a format very close to what the

Reader requires for displaying the fruit of your labour (or loins, if you're male).

Unlike the religious experience, eBook file conversion takes time, often as much time as producing the original master. There's nothing magical about it. You also have to *test* the file either on the Reader or via *emulator software* that pretends to be the Reader somewhere else, usually on your computer screen.

Like the religious version, eBook conversion is not for the faint-hearted. If you think of yourself as technology-challenged, or if using a remote control is an IQ test, you may need to ask for help to publish an eBook.

There may be a place for priests in the digital universe, after all.

5. Anyone can publish an eBook

True, but you need to get at the eMyth behind the Myth. Anyone can publish an eBook, but the trick is to do it well. (Anyone can dance, but some people's rendition of the Samba looks more like a violent vertical seizure!)

Years ago, after personal computers were invented, everyone suddenly had access to 301 fonts and used each of them to create and publish a book. Soon we nearly ran out of ISBNs and the world was no better off for the extra books that had been published. *Edit* became a nasty four-letter word and *proofreading* was something you hoped your best friend had done for your book before telling you it was the best thing since sliced cheese.

Tens of millions of books are available on the Kindle, Nook and Kobo Readers right now, but how many are worth reading?

We have a moral obligation to our National Library archives and time capsules everywhere to ensure that quality standards are kept up. You should still always lay your draft at the feet of an editor for advice, and a proofreader at the end of it all, before making an eBook of it. Your reputation as an author or publisher is at stake.

6. You design an eBook in much the same way as a print book

Up to a point, yes, but there are many twists and turns along the way in making it look as good as a physical book. You've already learned that the pdf file you prepare for print won't work on most Readers. You need to know what won't work in the Reader you're aiming to publish on.

For example, of the 301+ fonts available to you on your computer, only a handful will display on many Readers. You need to know what these Reader-friendly fonts are and what size to use in your original to ensure a proper display on the Reader. A 36 point title font, for example, will send most Readers ducking for cover.

Automatic features like page numbering, hyphenation and text placed in headers and footers will create special effects on many Readers, few of which you'll like. Extra line breaks and spacing between words in your original will cause chronic fatigue on most Readers.

7. One size fits all

There are companies out there that will promise to do everything for you for free and get your eBook onto every type of Reader from a single file you send them. Yes, but what will you get out the other end?

eBook Packagers like that may be well-intentioned, but none of them are charities. They depend on pushing large volumes of content through their system and getting it out there with a minimum of fuss. They may well have a 'muncher' that accepts any file type under the sun and then spits it out in multiple formats. But what it will look like at the other end is anyone's guess. If you read the small print, or ask the right questions, you'll find out that the formats they produce through this automated process will work on most but not all Readers, and certain types of content may not work at all, e.g. colour books and books in landscape format.

Never forget that *you* are the publisher and that *you* must take responsibility for what ultimately displays – or doesn't display – on the target Reader.

8. It costs less to publish an eBook than a print book

Yes, once you reach the print stage. With eBooks there are no upfront printing costs, no transport charges, no hassle with Customs if you print overseas, no warehousing, no physical distributors – or most other costs associated with a physical product.

But *pre-publication* costs of an eBook can be greater than a physical book, especially if you want to distribute your eBook via a wide range of Readers (see Myth 4).

With a print book you have ONE master file to check, perfect and send to print. With an eBook, you could have several versions, each of which has to be checked, perfected, tested offline and online, and then uploaded to a server where it *may* come out as you intended it.

Just because a process is handled by a computer doesn't make it idiot-proof. Sometimes, quite the opposite is true, especially if we become complacent.

9. Once you publish an eBook, you just sit back and wait for the royalty cheques to roll in

If you've ever published a print book, you know what a myth this is, so why should it be any different for eBooks?

Nothing's changed. You still have to get your book noticed, reviewed, blogged about. You also have to chat it up online, get interviewed. You have to send out email circulars, make sure it's listed on the key databases and high up on the search engines. Think in terms of a *campaign,* not a launch. Keeping your powder dry over several months. Thanks to virtual launches, you may be able to host your eBook in your pajamas – more on *that* later!

If anything, it's more challenging promoting an eBook. The world is just waking up to the eBook as a valid alternative to the printed book. People still like their physical books, even prefer them to eBooks. You'll need to persuade them not only to buy your book, but to accept it in digital wrapping.

Your audience will be well beyond your home suburb. They may not even speak your language. They are busier, more easily distracted, more constantly bombarded with distractions than readers have ever been. How will you meet them, introduce yourself and your work? Or convince them to buy?

You can be sure that no one else will do it for you – unless your work is the one in a million that captivates people into spreading it by word of mouth.

10. eBook contracts work pretty much like print book contracts

In some ways, yes. In many other areas, no. Conventional print book contracts are based on the notion of *territories.* You essentially lease your property to a publisher for a specified time and then have the right to take it back and lease it to someone else. If your work is commercial enough, you may be able to lease it to several publishers in several territories elsewhere in the world and make money from them as well as the original publisher.

But with eBooks, the notion of territory is mostly out the window. eBooks are *global* by nature rather than limited by geography. Their very existence undermines the territorial sanctity assigned to their physical counterparts. You may well find distributors that offer you territory-specific distribution, but how well they administer that arrangement, or police infringements, can be another matter.

Further, once published, eBooks have a half life approaching radioactive elements. It's hard enough to take down a physical book once it's on Amazon, and outlets all over the world are offering it new and used at various price points. Can you imagine how hard it will be to dismantle once it's up on multiple Readers? Or to cut off supply, if the hackers get into it and disable the digital rights protections?

The lawyers are working to counter that now. But the pace of legal evolution to meet the challenges of digital copyright and piracy will make *Bleak House* look like a sprint. In the meantime, all parties concerned will have to be on guard. Very much on guard!

1. An eBook is an eBook is an eBook

It isn't. eBooks come in all shapes and sizes. An eBook can comprise text on its own, or it can include images, sound, animation and even interactivity. What you can do with your eBook is limited only by your imagination. Or, if you plan to publish yourself, what you can do is limited by your technical expertise.

First, a bit of history. eBooks have actually been around for a long time. Ever since computers became as good at entering and saving text as punching numbers, people have been creating eBooks.

If you create a file and save it, you've made an electronic document. It may be a letter, a diary entry, a report, an essay, a story, or something even longer. The key difference between an electronic file and an eBook has to do with length and content, and what's done with it once it's created.

Few people would think a story five pages long would qualify as an eBook – unless it was very, *very* succinct – but a novella or a handbook of 40-50 pages might. And if the content can stand on its own and is of sufficient importance to be read as an independent document, it's probably an eBook if it remains in digital form – stored on a computer or floating around somewhere in cyberspace.

Does the act of printing change an eBook into something else? Probably. It's become *physical,* has claimed space on paper. It may be printed in quantity with a cover and sold in bookshops as a physical book. Does that spell the end of the digital file or eBook from which the physical book was created? No.

A book can have more than one life, and at least one of those lives can be in purely digital form. It may have more to say about the reader and their choice of reading channel. Old habits die hard!

But relax – we have nothing to fear from eBooks but fear itself. Almost everyone who has a computer has authored digital text files and probably informal eBooks in the past. You may not have *published* an eBook yet, but that's what we're getting at here.

Let's talk about the shape of eBooks.

First, consider the dimensions of the physical book. In theory, it can be any size, but there are practical limitations, like paper size and the capacity of presses to print on larger stock. If physical books are too large, bookshops and libraries may not be able to store them. And it rather defeats the romantic view of a book as something to curl up with in bed – even though some classical novels like *War and Peace* could qualify as lethal weapons by weight and bulk. So most publishers tend to publish using standard dimensions. Notable exceptions to this are picture books for kids and some 'coffee table' books intended for display rather than life in a bookcase.

eBooks in theory can also be of any size. As long as your eBook is set up to be viewed on a computer with a reasonable size monitor, it will be possible to view it, with scrolling, even if it doesn't fit the normal screen size.

Matters get complicated when publishers want to create eBooks from large format files using big fonts and images. There are many types of Readers out there, and many have small screen sizes, e.g. personal data assistants (PDAs) and 4G/LTE phones. It gets even more complicated when you want your eBook to be read – and legible – on the full range of eBook Readers.

The good news is that certain eBook software formats allow your text to flow properly into the various screen sizes used by the readers. The viewer then can resize the text to suit his or her viewing preferences, and then text reflows into the available space. This, too, is a subject we'll be looking at later – how we ensure the files we create will work on as many eBook readers as possible. More recently, formats have emerged for controlling the elements on the page so the eBook format works very much like the pdf. But there's a downside to these Fixed Layout Formats that we'll talk about later.

Many people think of eBooks as simply text on a screen. Early eBooks were just that, and the habit persists today with many publishers issuing eBooks versions of print books at the same time or even before the print versions are released. The viewing of digital text was, and still is, a problem. Few people want to read extended text on a backlit screen. Many people with vision problems simply couldn't read from the early devices. And, from an aesthetic point of view, people found it hard to curl up with a laptop or take it to the beach to read a novel.

Enter the dedicated eBook Reader. The first generation models solved the problem of portability, but their displays were either too dim or too bright for people to feel comfortable reading for a long time. They could generally only display text in one colour (black) and their storage space was very small. They didn't sell very well, weren't very robust, the market for eBooks took a dive, and many companies that had invested in eBook technology went bust.

Quite a few traditional publishers heaved a sigh of relief, thinking that the world – or at least theirs – had been saved from the dreaded eBook! Problem was, physical book sales continued to slump worldwide, except for notable exceptions like the Harry Potter series and vampire blockbusters. And the general cultural shift from the printed page to the screen for leisure and educational content continued. People were spending their time as viewers (TV and movie watchers) more often than as readers. Children – subject to dazzling multimedia content everywhere in their daily lives – were demanding more than text on a page from their reading experience. (If you could get them to pick up a book at all.)

It looked as if eBooks would have to have a second life if only to allow publishers to defend their market share against screen-based content. Second generation eBook readers were released, but they still suffered from limited storage, irritating back lighting and the difficulty of accessing and storing content. Sales continued to be very slow.

Several innovations have turned the tide. In 2007, Amazon released the first generation of their Kindle Reader, which supposedly sold out in five and a half hours. Clearly, Amazon had done their research: sales confirmed there was a market for a more sophisticated Reader whose only purpose was to display text on a screen. The Kindle had addressed the readability problem with an 'eInk' display that emulated the experience of reading a newspaper. It could handle pdf files natively, and it had direct access to Kindle books and the content supplied by Amazon partners like newspapers, who could download material to subscribers automatically from the internet.

Publishers sat up and took notice. At its release date, the Kindle Store claimed to have close to 90,000 titles onboard. At last count, the Store boasts more than several million titles (although Amazon has always been tight lipped about how many titles it actually sells). Statistics like that couldn't be ignored. Publishers began to factor eBooks into their production and marketing plans for titles, even releasing the Kindle version before the hardback of titles they expected to be bestsellers.

Several other companies have entered the fray from different angles. Technology companies like Sony and have produced dedicated Readers, Borders released their Kobo Reader, and 'open-source' multi-function devices like the iPad and Nook are also competing for market share. Smartphones like the iPhone, Blackberry and the Samsung Galaxy also can now download and display eBooks.

Feeling the heat, Amazon released a third generation Reader in 2009. It also released Kindle for PC, software that made it possible for customers to download Kindle books for reading on their PC and-via special apps (applications) like Stanza-onto 3G devices like the iPhone. Amazon continues to be competitive with its new Kindle Fire range of colour devices.

Even more recently, Apple threw down the gauntlet to Amazon by releasing their iPad, which accesses content from Apple's iBookstore. The iPad, and competing 'tablet' devices, display not only text but also files enhanced with multimedia elements like audio, video and animation. Multimedia-rich pdfs can now play on these tablets and smartphones.

Which brings us back to the original question of what an eBook is, or rather what it will shape-change to become.

Viewers are becoming more demanding of their devices. The ideal device should be able to play audio and video files while the viewer is reading text, and offer at least basic interactivity like the ability to mark up content, add notes, or even provide feedback to the publisher. (Imagine how the reading of *Moby Dick* could be enhanced by the sound of the ocean in the background.)

The iPad can play multimedia elements in full colour, as long as the files it downloads have those features on board. But Apple and other distributors continue to rule out the pdf as the preferred format for *delivering* content to its iBookstore. Why? Probably because pdf files are significantly larger than other formats, even without multimedia. They take more space to store on servers and on portable devices, and would take longer to download.

The problem is further complicated by the diversity of software formats required by devices out there. Companies like Amazon saw having their own format as preferable to 'open source' ones. A lot of this has to do with jockeying for position in the marketplace.

The good news is that hardware companies like Sony have opened up their Readers to accept pdfs and open source publishing formats like ePub. Essentially a compressed file in a web-based format similar to html, ePub will work on almost all readers, with the notable exception of the Kindle. It's the delivery packaging preferred by Apple and other major eBook aggregators and distributors.

But efficiency isn't everything: earlier versions of ePub didn't accept multimedia enhancements other than colour and graphics. Nor does it allow for precise control of the way pages display. More recent updates to the ePub format (currently ePub3, introduced in 2012) do allow for inclusion of multimedia elements, though whether or not the eBook display will play them is another matter. More importantly, Fixed Layout ePub (flePub) files now allow for layout control in books that rely on two page spreads, such as art books, children's picture books and some text books.

While the bits and pieces are coming together, the trick will be finding a way to load these enhancements onto software that the big distributors of content will accept, and that most reading devices can play.

Recently, Apple released an application, iBooks Author. This program allows multimedia elements to be integrated into the eBook master via "widgets" and to play from within that file – at least in the Apple environment. Barnes & Noble are providing a conversion service to publishers that will allow their children's books to be read aloud on their Nook devices. To compete with the iPad and other tablets' ability to zoom via a swipe of the fingers, devices such as the Kindle Fire and Nook support magnification of certain areas on the page, which can be helpful, especially in children's books.

In short, what an eBook *can* be on the drawing board or in a design studio is probably less important for individual and small publishers at present than what can be efficiently and economically delivered to market.

Publishers with titles they expect to have a reasonable shelf life could decide to develop and archive enhanced files via "future proofed" formats such as xml. Hopefully, the big hardware and software companies will soon find a way to integrate enhancements into existing software like ePub, or develop new software that is consistently multimedia-friendly.

In the short term, publishers can offer enhanced eBooks for download from their own sites as html5 or ePub3, or pdf files. In the case of more dynamic content, offering Flash videos or Quicktime movies for internet streaming or download might be best. Audio books in mp3 are widely accepted by global companies such as CD Baby and Content Reserve (Overdrive), who distribute to more than 30 online audio stores such as iTunes and Audible.com.

2. One eBook Reader is much the same as another

Some are, some aren't. eBook Readers (i.e. reading devices) come in all shapes and sizes. The Kindle, iPad, Nook and Kobo and a few others are relatively BIG. Smartphones like the iPhone are small. In response to, or perhaps anticipating, market demand, some tablets are getting smaller, while certain smartphones are getting bigger.

They have varying amounts of real estate on their screens for displaying your content. Some can display landscape (wide) as well as in portrait (tall) format. So, if you like to create wide content, you may have problems displaying it on a portrait Reader. Or, it may display but be unreadable except for those with magnifying glasses.

Most Readers can display colour, while older and cheaper models only black and white.

Some are excellent at displaying images; others aren't much better at that than a fax machine.

Some can play audio and even movies, or connect to the internet, while others do only static stuff and only connect to the internet to take your money when you buy a book.

The Maxi End of Town

You'd have to have be Rip Van Winkle not to have noticed how Apple Inc, Amazon, Kobo and Barnes & Noble have faced off with each of their own top-of-the-range Readers.

Amazon struck first with their Kindle 2, the second generation ***Kindle DX,*** and the ***Kindle DX International Edition.*** The Kindle DX International Edition is of greatest interest to viewers outside of North America, because it actually *works* in countries besides the USA through its 'global wireless' system.

All Kindles now come armed with wireless 4G/LTE and Wi-Fi connectivity, which means you don't have to be hooked up to a wired network at home or at the office to browse for books. Once you've downloaded your books via their ***Whisper-net*** gateway, you can work offline – which is true for all Readers, cheap or expensive.

While the smaller Kindles still mix it up with the majority of other Readers of similar size, having a mere 15.4cm (6") diagonal viewing area, the largest Kindle models offer a whopping 24.5cm (9.7") diagonal area. With the display default setting, this still isn't large enough to view two newspaper columns side by side, but it's not bad. Straight text files can be resized manually and automatically reflow to fit your available screen-estate.

The Kindle also offers 'text-to-speech', which is certainly not the same as a proper audio version of a book-as anyone who has been tortured by automated call centre monologues can attest-but it can be helpful for reading impaired people.

The Kindles support pdf files and can even display them in landscape as well as portrait format. But anyone who wants to take notes or highlight what they're reading at the same time will find it frustrating because the keyboard is physical rather than virtual, so it doesn't shift when you turn the device.

The Kindle has been hyped up as a portable text book library. At this stage, though, the prices of etextbooks aren't all that much cheaper – at least in North America – than their physical paper counterparts, so this prediction may be a bit premature. This could be due to the higher production costs faced by educational publishers to covert their works into formats like xhtml that will work on the Kindle – not a trivial passtime, as you'll see later on.

The only type of colour that the eInk Kindles will display is web-based content when you're browsing for books, and downloaded pdf files such as colour magazines to which you have a subscription.

The latest generation Kindles can now handle multimedia elements, but there still seems to be a lag between the capability of the devices and the delivery system of amazon.com.

The ***iPad*** and some of the recent Android tablets remain a special case, somewhere between a laptop, netbook, eBook Reader and a smartphone. It has on board most of the multimedia features you get on a laptop *plus* those you expect with a smartphone and more – except, of course, the phone itself. The premium model has double the storage capacity (64Gb) of any current eBook Reader. Not only will the iPad play audio and video, it plays them at Home Theatre quality. And you can browse the net and network via its touch screen while immersing yourself in the multimedia experience. If you get lost while browsing, the iPad, like the iPhone, has an onboard GPS that will help get you home physically or virtually. The iPad also has the ability to take, edit and distribute photos and videos via integrated software such as iPhoto, iMovie and Garageband. Properly set up, it can even 'find itself' if it gets lost or stolen!

Now in its third generation, the iPad continues to test the limits of what a portable device can do, blurring the distinction between the tablet and laptop in terms of features and functionality.

Powered by the Google Android OS, tablets like the Nook and Kobo are challenging Apple's dominance of the market, giving consumers greater choice and more affordable devices.

To rival the Amazon Kindle Store, Apple has set up the iBookstore. Akin to the iTunes Store, the iBookstore allows you to browse, sample and download books, store them on your iPad and sync them to your iPhone or your Mac computer automatically. Mac users have an App Store widget on their Dock, which whisks them off to the latest displays of software and apps, which will doubtlessly include transmedia (text + audio + video) books. Other competitors like Google, Kobo and Barnes & Noble have their own shops, with similar connectivity with Android and even Apple powered devices.

The Micro End of Town

There are a dizzying number of smartphone models out there, but the market seems to focusing its attention on Apple's iPhone, the Blackberry, and other brands that employ the Google Android operating system, most notably the Samsung Galaxy S III. Since the release of the iPhone 4, Apple's market share has continued to rise, and after a brief pause before the release of the iPhone 5, it is expected to regain its position as market leader.

It's questionable how many people actually use their phones' capability to read whole eBooks, but improvements in screen resolution make this more feasible for people preferring compact devices when they're on the go. Certainly, people are already using smartphones to access their magazines and newspaper issues on subscription. Social networking sites are now accessed more often via smartphone than via PC. Businesses such as the major banks have developed smartphone-specific apps to streamline their users' online visits. Some sites allow viewers to pick up content on their smartphone from where they left off at home on their computer or tablet.

As for file formats, smartphones can handle optimized pdfs as well as enriched eBook formats. The free Stanza application enables iPhone users to download and view Kindle files. Several well-heeled companies such as Simon & Schuster are developing specific apps to enable iPhones to view multimedia titles downloaded from the iBookstore. As mentioned earlier, Apple's reluctance to integrate Flash movie support will act as a brake on development of .swf enriched titles; and fewer people now use Flash.

The trend seems to be away from hardware-specific software formats for particular phones, preferring open source formats, or bridging software that can read a range of formats, such as Adobe Digital Editions (ADE) and Calibre. However, these packages don't always live up to their promise. For example, because Adobe applies digital rights management (DRM) protection that isn't compatible with the iPhone's Stanza app, ADE processed files won't work on iPhones. Even Stanza, which was developed for the iPhone, currently has problems syncing files between the iPad and iPhone, so viewers who start reading on an iPad at home may not be able to sync the same file to their iPhone to continue reading on the train.

The point to be mindful of here is that it may take years for consistent standards in eBook Readers and software to emerge, if they ever do. Publishers may well look back with nostalgia on the conventional printing process, where a single press-ready pdf was processed by pdf-friendly printers to yield predictable results. In the meantime, publishers and distributors will have to juggle content between several formats to ensure global coverage, and archive all their masters in order for conversion to format standards that haven't been invented yet.

Who said that eBook publishing would be easier?

3. Once you create a pdf, do you have an eBook?

Once upon a time, publishing was easy. You scratched out a story on the walls of a cave and left it for passersby to view exactly as you created it. Not content with a finite readership, one author decided to record his thoughts on media that could be moved – the bark of trees and such. Perhaps the original went down so well with the first few people who read it that the author decided to make copies and engage a distributor. From that point on, he was on a slippery slope to either bestsellerdom or oblivion.

Readers became attached to reading bestsellers on bark. There was something romantic about curling up with your own slab of bark and smelling the Great Outdoors as you read. But so much bark was used up that the trees began to die and someone chanced on chipping the dying trees for their pulp and inventing paper. Readers didn't see the point. Paper would never replace bark. Paper was, well, *flat* and it reflected light outdoors and hurt your eyes...

It hasn't got any better recently.

The age of real printing-of typewriters and cameras, and leading made out of lead, film and metal plates-was two steps forward and one step back. It did not promote trust between authors, publishers and printers. Authors felt that publishers would change important things in their books behind their backs with half a chance, and both groups mistrusted printers who often would 'improve' work out of recognition.

Computers actually made things worse. Publishers went out of their way to have better or at least different types of computers from their authors, with software that wouldn't speak to the author and fonts that had a mind of their own, especially when they were teleported between computers. Printers took no responsibility beyond photographing and immortalising any mistakes between the author and publisher. They didn't hesitate to charge sometimes horrendous fees to fix up things after the fact.

Enter *postscript language.* This was a coding that no author, publisher or printer really understood. It embedded fonts in a file so that they couldn't be changed by a subversive act. Suddenly there was peace in fonts between computers.

But this wasn't enough. Page layout could change from the author's computer to the publisher's and again on the printer's.

Enter the *pdf* (portable document format), which froze each page like a snapshot so that, no matter whether you were Mac or PC, your file would look the same on the next computer down the food chain. (Sound the heraldic trumpets!) Adobe Acrobat was the Messiah of the publishing world. Authors, publishers and printers all became friends again. What you gave the printer was exactly what appeared in print. *Almost* exactly. Most of the time.

Enter the eBook. Or, as we've learned in the first two chapters, the *eBooks.*

Pdfs are fine for porting computer to computer, or even from computer directly to some eBook Readers.

But not all. The pdf prefers to be planted and blossom in place. It does not like being exported to other format environments.

Because pdfs have every bit of information you would ever need about a file and probably more, they tend to be chunky. And bigger is *not* always better in the eBook world. Big takes too long to upload and just as long to download. Big takes too much space to store on servers for online stores, even in a storage 'cloud'. Big may be precise, reliable, even beautiful, but it doesn't work in a world where efficiency and speed are paramount.

Publishers and authors need to unlearn that pdfs are the end of the workflow if they want to go digital. If you hold a press-ready pdf of your work in hand, you have already gone further than necessary to publish an eBook. You'll need to update your publishing GPS (Global Publishing System!) and remake your file to make it acceptable for eBook conversion.

What follows may be counter-intuitive to those used to worshipping on bended knee in the temple of the pdf, but the instructions are essential if you are to publish eBooks.

Take notes from now on. *Please.*

First there was the Word

It used to be that we revised a manuscript at several stages. We took it as far as we could in Microsoft Word, or other text editing programs, and then perfected it in InDesign or Quark (the page layout programs) before exporting it as a press-ready pdf and sending it out into the world. It was a single-lane highway, with pit-stops along the way and no U-turns. Forward, never back – did you get that down in your notes?

What's wrong with this scenario, as we've already learned, is that if we rely on the perfect pdf and bin the almost perfect Word file along the way, we'll be in trouble. eBook files are not instantly made from pdfs or Indesign or Quark files, or even Word files, but Word – or Pages on the Mac – may be closer to the mark than InDesign or the Acrobat pdf.

There are conversion programs that supposedly change pdfs to ePub files or xhtml files at the click of a button, but the results are often not pretty. When you see them, you may well be tempted to start from scratch.

What you may see before you is an unruly mass of text. Heading styles may be ignored. Whole passages may be misplaced. Graphics and photos may be jettisoned to the end of the file or to some invisible parallel universe. Those font choices you made in agony have been ignored in favour of 'default' eBook-friendly ones. Line breaks are ignored or put in seemingly at random. Photographs already lovingly Photoshopped are arbitrarily reversed out.

If you conclude that much of the time you spent setting up Styles in Word and fine-tuning them in InDesign was wasted, you'll be mostly right. You can set up Styles in the xhtml file but they won't be Word styles. You can set up Styles in ePub, but they won't be your InDesign ones.

To preserve your sanity, you have two choices. First, you can insist on making Word the place where you perfect your editorial work or perhaps make last minute changes to both the Word and InDesign files – now don't forget any! Or you can do your perfecting in InDesign and then export (read, go backwards) to a rich text format (.rtf) version for Word and/or ePub and/or xml/xhtml. The latter two options, as we'll see, are your best choices.

Got that?

Keep in mind that exporting from InDesign is not the end of the story but rather the beginning of a new one. You'll still have to adjust the layout and styles for eBook viewing.

From Word/rtf you may be able to apply Word styles exported from InDesign, or recreate and apply the styles you want again. This means more editorial and proofreading work of the design, but at least you can rely on the text to be perfect. Or can you?

Exporting to xml/xhtml, you'll find yourself designing and laying out with your favourite web editing package – oh, joy! You'll have access to web friendly fonts and CSS styles much more limited than what you're used to in Word. Thank your lucky stars that the file isn't filled with concrete poetry and aberrant extra character spaces. Oops, it is?

And then there's the dedicated eBook format, ePub, another export choice available to you from InDesign. If you have a decent ePub editing program like *Sigil,* what you start with from the exported file may look pretty good, but you'll still have to fine-tune it.

More on the detail of actual conversions in the next chapter.

Bye, bye pdfs?

So, after all this, is there any reason to create pdfs for eBooks? Possibly, but only in the short term.

Remember that the pdf format was invented to embed fonts and graphics in a file and ensure it looks the same at the other end as the original. It's unlikely that the way files display on eBook Readers will ever be exact replicas of the original, and few viewers other than paper vendors and unemployed printers will be all that concerned about it. Most eBook Readers are more about efficiency and functionality than aesthetics.

Pdfs do have a role to play in compensating for the limitations of current eBook software formats and expanding the horizon for what is possible in future eBooks. Readers that can play multimedia enriched pdfs like the iPad will be more attractive to consumers than those with more static displays. Adobe Creative Suite (which contains Acrobat) does have the ability to produce optimized pdf files from InDesign masters, as required by Adobe Digital Editions (ADE) software. These pdfs can contain enhancements like mp3/mp4 audio, and video files such as Quicktime and Flash movies. But remember that Flash movies don't play on some Apple devices.

These standalone pdfs are a cost-effective alternative to the special apps some publishers are creating for high volume works (see Chapter 2). But I predict that they'll soon be redundant. There are already apps on the market, most notably Apple's iBooks Author, that theoretically do it all for you, without you needing to write a single line of code. Bless you, Apple! But that's a conditional thanks, as you'll see...

While you're waiting for further break-throughs, you may be interested in seeing how IP's Digital Publishing Centre (DPC) composes multimedia enriched pdfs for our titles (we were doing this before ePubs came on the scene). The process is surprisingly straightforward – at least once you've done it once or twice!

Here's what you need to get started:

- A fairly recent computer (obviously!).
- A fairly recent version of Word (nothing earlier than 97, please!). Or Mac users can use Pages and then export to Word. Open Office/Neo Office users can save to .doc and still be in the game.
- A fairly recent version of Adobe's *Creative Suite* (I'll be describing what happens with CS6, the Suite's latest incarnation). The apps you'll especially need will be InDesign, Acrobat, and possibly Distiller. Photoshop is desirable but not essential-any decent image editing program that allows for optimizing graphics and photos will suffice. Beware of "light" or "express" products that don't have this ability. If you've already invested in QuarkXpress, the other top-end design and layout program, you'll probably be OK, but the functions you need may be in different places from where they're at in InDesign, and I don't pretend to be a Quark expert.
- *iTunes.* This is a free download from Apple so there's no reason not to have it, and it makes it really easy to convert your audio to something you can include in your pdfs.
- Patience!

The Next Word

Obviously, first up we need to produce an InDesign master. At IP we start with the master we've already prepared for conventional print, if we're producing a print version and an eBook. If you've already printed the work conventionally, you probably have a master you can work with; otherwise you'll have to produce one by importing your text into InDesign and laying it out. Seek professional advice if you haven't done this before and your eyes are starting to glaze over.

In the pdf you're going to author, you'll give viewers the choice of having the audio file(s) play automatically when they open the main file, or when they open the page where the audio clip lives.

If you want to give the viewer the choice of listening to audio or not, you'll need to to add audio buttons in your InDesign file. From them, we'll link to audio clips that you'll publish along with the text file.

You can design your own Play button in Photoshop or simply cut and paste a clipart one into InDesign. Word has a handy clipart button that we use. Once you've created or imported one instance of your audio button, you can copy and paste it anywhere else in the InDesign file where it's needed.

This workflow is ideal for individual stories or poems where you want to link the text to individual audio files. The same approach works for video files you want to play along with the text, but remember my earlier advice about pdfs you plan to send to the iBookstore – no Flash movies allowed, only Apple-friendly Quicktime!

Once your audio or video play buttons have been placed in the InDesign file, you'll need to produce a postscript file that a sub-program of InDesign called Distiller will use to create your pdf file. You can export directly to pdf from InDesign, but Distiller gives you a wider range of choice for the type of pdf you'll create, and some eBook distributors demand you send them particular rather than generic pdf files created in the background by using the Export to command in InDesign.

To create a postscript file from the InDesign master:

1. Go to File/Print.
2. Select Postscript File as the Printer. This is a virtual printer that will produce a .ps (postscript) file you'll use in Distiller.
3. Save this in a separate folder so you can find it easily. Postscript files have .ps as the file name suffix, as opposed to .indd (Indesign)
4. Open Distiller.
5. At the top drag down window, select PDF/A-1b:2005 (RGB), the standard expected by Adobe Digital Editions.
6. Drag in your .ps file and let Distiller do the job it's been paid to do.
7. Put the outputted pdf file in another folder you'll be able to find later.
8. *Voilá* – you now have a master pdf. Wasn't that easy?

You now need to convert and import your audio or video files. The process is similar for both, so I'll just show you what to do with audio files.

Your original files may be .aif or some other Windows stereo designation like .wav. If you are recording your own audio, do so at the highest possible quality.

This avoids having to spend hours or days in postproduction trying to fix things that would have been fine if your recording equipment had been better or the recording space had been properly set up in the first place.

You can then convert the files to mp3 or mp4 (also know as AAC) files. Use iTunes to easily convert stereo files to compressed formats this way:

1. Open iTunes.
2. Go to Preferences/General/Import Settings.
3. Choose either mp3 or mp4. mp3 is safer, but mp4 produces slightly higher quality files.
4. Import your audio files into iTunes.
5. Under the Advanced menu, choose convert. Select whatever audio compression format you selected under Preferences, e.g. mp3. iTunes does the hard work, placing the converted files under the originals in the window.
6. Drag the converted files into a new folder, labeling them by track number, i.e. 01, 02, etc.
7. Place this audio folder in the same folder as your pdf master. *Very important:* once you have placed the audio folder in position, do not move it!
8. Go back to your pdf master and navigate to each audio icon, selecting the Sound Tool under the Advanced Menu, then linking it to the appropriate audio file in your mp3 or mp4 folder.
9. Tell Acrobat to create a player that the viewer can use to start the audio, pause it and adjust the volume control. Do this for each audio file in

turn. Go to Tools/Multimedia/Sound. This brings up a window that allows you to define the size of the player, whether it's fixed to the page and whether it plays automatically when the page is opened, or requires the viewer to click on the player.

10. Test your master offline BEFORE sending it off anywhere!

At the end of the process, you'll have a multimedia enhanced pdf that can be played in most eBook Readers that accept pdfs, or even burnt to CD/DVD for physical distribution. The tricky part is delivering that file to the customer as a download. Quite a few distributors do not distribute even optimized pdfs, and even fewer distribute pdfs with multimedia elements in them. Until that changes - if it ever does - your customers will have to get the file from you directly.

As I said, it's easy to do this once you've done it once or twice, but, if it all seems too hard, you can always get the Digital Publishing Centre, or your own multimedia designer, to create the enhanced pdf for you.

If you decide to outsource elsewhere, you'll need to supply your designer with the master InDesign file and your master audio folder. Check with him/her for the proper way to package your InDesign master before sending it off.

4. Is Conversion a religious experience?

In an ideal world, you'd be able to press a single button to make your book into an eBook. But Heaven on Earth isn't here – yet. Nor is it likely that The Rapture will be arriving any time soon. The problem is that the major distributors of eBook content want to maximise their profits in what they still see as a risky area of business. They want to attract customers to their site and keep them coming back. But, if customers are empowered with *choice,* if they can shop around, they might not come back. What better way to maintain customer 'loyalty' than by selling them an eBook Reader that only works with your content?

Fortunately there are only a finite number of eBook formats out there (at last count), and certain 'open-source' Readers can handle several formats. The Nook is one such Reader.

Key Formats

The problem for publishers, whether they are multinationals or individuals, is knowing which formats they need to release for their titles to reach the largest possible audience. Not too long ago, some publishers contented themselves with the xhtml format required by Amazon to upload for the Kindle, which in turn became the .mobi file. They accepted the Amazon hype that the only eBooks worth having were ones available on the Kindle. While Amazon continues to sell more eBooks than most of its competitors combined, it may not always be so, and publishers are wisely covering several bases in their preparation of their eBooks.

Publishers can cover most bases by producing an optimized pdf, an xhtml (.mobi, or more recently KF8), and an ePub version of each title.

That may be good news for the new players on the block, but not for publishers seeking that elusive single eBook workflow solution. Not only do publishers have yet another channel to feed (the iBookstore, Kobo, Google and Barnes & Noble), but they also have a different format requirement to deal with: the ePub. The ePub seems to be the format of choice for open source eBook Readers and tablets.

We've already seen how easy it is to produce a pdf (review your notes!), even an enriched one, if you have the right software and a bit of patience. But what about the other format versions?

Keep in mind that xhtml and ePub – at least in its ePub2 edition – are not formats intended to produce multimedia-rich titles, but rather text with few graphics. The most recent incarnations (KF8 and ePub3) may allow you to integrate some multimedia into your file, but there are no guarantees that this content will play on all Readers, or be distributable by your distributors of choice. Your main purpose for an ePub is to create a file with text and possibly some images that will work in most Readers.

So what are the features of these new formats? Both xhtml and ePub are optimized, that is, able to embed and display images that have been compressed by means of image editors like Photoshop. xhtml is a derivative from the html (hypertext markup language) used for website and blog authoring. Both have the ability to 'talk' to eBook devices as well as browsers on your computer, to convert coded text and graphics into visible text and graphics. But ePub is more actively being refined as the best open source format for delivery of eBook content. For now, anyway!

Converting from Print to Digital formats

Both xhtml and ePub formats can be output from InDesign, using the File/Export To command. When dealing with an xhtml file, you'll need to refine it with a web editor, which makes sense because it's mostly web-based coded content. The styles you can use or set up will be CSS (cascading style sheets), which is the closest you'll get to normal Word styles in this environment. If you know something about code and still are not afraid of it, you can create your own set of CSS styles to make the xhtml file look *almost* as good as the original, but don't get too excited: the meat-grinder software at the eBook distributor's end may still change that to something more standard that most Readers can display.

Once you have your master xhtml file, you'll probably want to send it to Amazon for the Kindle, but you may not be able to do this. You'll first have to ***register with Amazon*** to become a content provider, and there are no guarantees that you'll be accepted, although the Club is becoming less and less exclusive these days. It helps to have a US address and a US bank account – but more on that in the chapter where I talk about getting paid. The other alternative is to use a third party 'aggregator' who will do it all for you and either charge you an upfront fee and/or take a share of the royalties, which in turn is a share of what they get back from Amazon. Again, more on that later.

As I said, with ePub, you'll need special ePub editor software to deal with what InDesign serves up in export. There are several around, but we like *Sigil.* It's free, open-source and it seems to work. Best of all, you can convert html and text (txt) files to ePub right in the program. The interface looks almost like a stripped down text editor, which it is – sort of. It provides you with folders in which you can store your project fonts, images and even styles to process your file. It comes equipped with ePub essentials like Chapter Break commands, so that the display Reader knows when to start a new page. It also has options for bolding, italicizing, underlining and resizing your text. It even has a validator, which will preflight your file for errors and point you to the place that needs fixing.

In theory, you can make your ePub version look almost the same as the original, but caution is advised here.

Most Readers, especially the smartphones, have problems with font sizes larger than 16pt. And keep in mind here that certain fonts display larger in 16pt than others. So I would advise that you not get too dramatic or creative with your headings; otherwise you may find them taking up a full screen on some devices.

The key thing to remember when converting and editing ePub and xhtml files is to be *conservative* in your selection of fonts, your line spacing, and spacing between words, especially if you're poetically inclined. What you think you're getting away with in Sigil may result in unpleasant surprises on a Reader.

Enter *Calibre.* Another free software program, it advertises itself as your "one-stop solution to all your eBook needs". Where have we heard that before? While it is certainly an elegant program, it's not *everything* you need – unless you have a straightforward file for conversion. Where Calibre shines is as an emulator, and as a local conduit of content from your computer to your portable Reader. First it lets you view your file in a variety of formats as it will appear on certain Readers such as the Kindle or Sony Reader. It also can convert from many formats to other formats, but it freely admits that it's better at handling certain formats than others. The good old pdf is at the bottom of the pecking order. If you didn't hear my advice before, it's NOT a good idea to create ePub or other eBook formats from a pdf.

Outsourcing

If you're a publisher, like IP, you're probably receving daily pitches from tech companies in India, China and elsewhere. These companies usually offer not only to provide conversions for you, but also to create apps for your title, so all its multimedia bells and whistles will work on more sophisticated devices like the iPad. These companies offer to convert your files from Word, .rtf, InDesign or even pdf to ePub, xhtml and other eBook formats specific to certain Readers like the Blackberry and Palm. They tend to charge by the page and by the format, and the prices vary from 20 cents US per page to 30 cents or more. The lower prices are for titles that are straightforward, with minimal photos, graphics, tables, etc. The higher prices are for more complex, graphic-intensive titles.

While I would suggest you do your own research on these companies before sending them your files, one possible place to begin your comparisons is with ***Aptara.*** They're US-based but may outsource some functions. They also sponsor informative web seminars about the currents trends in e-publishing, which gives the impression they're not in it just for a quick buck.

For you poets out there, the news is good: a 100 page book will only cost you about US $25 to convert per format. Sometimes you can get a discount if you get them to produce more than one format. However, if you're an author of fantasy tomes, you could be paying US $100 or more per format. Time to get concise?

Fine-tuning

Keep in mind, too, that there's no guarantee that the eBook file will come back pristine and ready to upload to your distribution partner as is. You'll need to do a design proof and probably run it through Sigil to make any changes, or be prepared to play email tag with the conversion people until they get it right. How much time do you have?

The other point to keep in mind is that eBook distributors have different specifications for the files to be sent. They want to be sure that your file will work in the maximum number of devices without a problem, which is understandable, so the best way to ensure that this will happen is to tell you what features your ePub or other format file must adhere to. If you ignore the specs, your file may well be rejected, causing further delays until you can get it fixed.

So, before you get a hired gun to produce your files for you, I would strongly suggest that you send them the specs from the distributors you plan to use, and get them to agree to produce files that pass the specs tests before you hand over any money.

Another third-party option is to have the distributor convert or arrange conversions of your file. Chapters/Indigo in North America (known as Borders in Australia) have partnered with ***Kobo,*** the same company that produces the Kobo Reader mentioned already. You can send them files in almost any format, including the dreaded pdf, and they'll convert it to ePub for you. Their pricing structure is a bit different, though. Basic files cost US $29 to convert up to 215 pages. Thereafter they charge about 15 cents per page. This is a bit more expensive for the impoverished poets wanting to e-publish their precious chapbook, but good news for the tomers.

As part of the Kobo deal, you get the ePub file sent to you to do with as you will later on, which means you can upload it to other eBook distributors. Kobo also offers distribution through Borders/Chapters/Indigo, but read the small print before you sign. I'll discuss distribution options in greater detail in Chapter 7.

OK. You've got your new eBook format in your hand. What's next? You have to get it out there, but there are a confusing number of channels you could choose. How do you know which one or ones to pick? I'll address that in Chapter 8.

Let's summarise what we've learned in this chapter.

- The eBook industry still hasn't sorted out a single format that will work with all Readers, and they're not likely to do so any time soon.
- Readers vary in terms of the eBook format they can handle. Some will display some features of the eBook file but not all.
- You need to create eBook format files that have the best chance of working in as many Readers as possible.
- You can convert the files yourself via free software packages, or you can pay someone else to do it, but you are still ultimately responsible for ensuring everything displays as you intended it to.
- The best advice is to test your files before you publish, using an emulator like Calibre and Adobe Digital Editions, and take advantage of any preview options offered by the distributor.

The last point has to do with Quality Control – a big issue with eBooks. But the process of ensuring the work looks as professional as possible begins much earlier in the process. Check out the next chapter.

5. Keeping it Real: Quality Control

Yes! Anyone can publish an eBook. In fact anyone can be a publisher of eBooks. You don't need a Ph.D in Creative Writing or a Diploma in Publishing – you can just *do it.*

The scenario looks like this:

You get a computer with a text editing program.

You sign up for a broadband account.

You wait for inspiration to hit you (or you ambush it).

You write the book.

You run it through the spell-checker (if you have time).

You let the editing program auto-correct any mistakes.

You think of a catchy title for the book.

You think of a catchy name for your publishing company.

You register as publisher with an online distributor or distributors.

You upload your book.

You wait for pay cheques to roll in.

Congratulations! You're a 'self-publisher'. You don't need a publisher to validate the worth of what you've written, do you? You don't need a distributor to agree that your book has commercial potential. You've exercised your democratic right to publish your work to the world and let the market decide!

But what's wrong with this scenario?

Not much, really, on the face of it. You've put your book out there and claimed your space on at least one virtual bookshelf, cover (rather than spine) out. If you've published it as an eBook, you've harmed no one, even if no one buys your book, and you haven't wasted any precious resources or added to global warming by printing physical books and having to pulp the ones that don't sell.

But will your eBook succeed? How many people will have to buy it before you consider it a success? And if they don't download it in droves, will you have your excuses ready?

There are, in fact, many reasons why books don't sell, and few of them have much to do with bad luck. Poor promotion. Poor distribution choices. Unfair competition from other publishers. Lack of interest in the marketplace. I'll talk about some of those external factors in later chapters. But there is one factor that is firmly in the control of the author and publisher that can have an impact on a book's success, be it an eBook or a physical one...

Quality control. Editorial. Design. Production.

These are terms you may have heard about, even tried your hand at. But will you be able to resist the temptation to shortcut past them in a digital environment, where it's so easy to send your book straight to market? Isn't that what self-publishing is all about – DIY?

Let's make one thing clear at this point. And if you don't accept what I say, you might as well skip to the next chapter, because there won't be much in the rest of this chapter for you.

For 99.327% of the population, self-publishing is a misnomer. Most people simply aren't equipped to do everything that needs to be done in order to publish an excellent book by themselves. You may be a good author, but perhaps you lack the editorial skills to refine your work. Or you may be a good editor but still be unable to view your work objectively enough to properly edit it. You may have a flair for design and think you know how to design your book cover. And you may think you can pick up the skills to prepare your book for e-publication and distribution on the fly. But can you?

I've published 24 titles now, and some of these have been published by IP. Does that make me a self-publisher? In some ways, yes. But I would never dare to do it all myself.

I have reasonably good skills as an author and designer and not bad skills as an editor, but I rely on other readers to edit and proofread my work before it gets to design stage. I see the writing and publication process as a collaborative one, where I have to involve people outside the project to help me refine it, indeed to advise me whether it's worthwhile publishing at all.

The relative ease of e-publishing is a dangerous thing. Frustrated by rejection slips from an increasingly selective bunch of publishers, some people will decide to self-publish. They may not consciously shortcut the process. They may not know what needs to be done to ensure their book is up to publishable standard. But they owe it to themselves, to the market and the world, to become informed about the critical stages each book needs to go through before it's released, in whatever form.

These steps will be commonsense to experienced authors. But even they may need reminding that not much has changed in preparing a book for e-publication over the conventional book. You should feel guilty if you skip or rush any of the stages below. *Very* guilty!

Here they are:

Concept

There are some books that really shouldn't be published for the market place, books that are doomed to fail before they are written. Get advice from agents, assessors, editors, booksellers, librarians, and objective readers before spending a year writing a book that only a few people will read, such as Aunt Miriam's Memoirs. With such advice, you may be able to redo your concept into a workable one. Or you may need to go back to the drawing – or authoring – board.

Once you've done that, test your idea again, and be prepared to modify it into something that has a chance of attracting attention as a book.

First drafts and other reality checks

Similar to Concept, here you consider a mid-course correction. Has your idea panned out in written form? Have you strayed from the workable concept into an unworkable one? Are you still on track to deliver the promise of your concept? Return to the groups mentioned under Concept for a second opinion. If you don't have an agent, consider paying for a professional assessment by a qualified assessor who has credentials in your writing area (ask for references!).

Content and copy edits

This is a common stage where you might be tempted to cut corners. People who think a work can be properly edited in one go are deluding themselves.

The first type of edit, structural editing, looks at big picture issues such as continuity, coherence, logic, consistency, and factual accuracy. It can take several redrafts to get these aspects working properly for you.

The second type, copy editing, looks at micro-issues like sentence structure, idiom, voice, person, mechanics, and ensuring the work has flow. It takes a special kind of editor to do content and copy editing, and most editors are better at one than the other.

Resist the temptation to have your spouse or close friend do either type of editing for you, even if they have experience. There should be nothing personal about the editorial process. Be prepared to submit your work for more than one assessment to cover all these aspects with a specialist's guidance.

Proofreading

While proofreaders are often skilled at copy editing, it does take a special eye to catch the uncatchables in a manuscript that's already been edited several times. A good way of proofreading is to read the manuscript aloud. A better way to proofread is to read the manuscript aloud to someone who is reading it along with you. This was a tried-and-true method used by many conventional publishers before budgets and other distractions led them to seek less costly methods of proofing.

Design proofing

A sub-set of proofreading, but well worth mentioning here, especially for would-be eBook publishers, is design proofing. WYSIWYG (what you see is what you get) is a term that applies to a comparison of documents viewed on a screen with what you get when they are printed out. The ideal WYSIWYG system gives you exactly in print what you see on the screen. But it's much more difficult to get WYSIWYG between a computer screen and an eBook Reader, because, as we've already learned, there are so many different devices out there. The way they display eBook content can vary depending on how you send them your content and how that content is displayed on their device.

As a design proofer, then, your job is to ensure you put your file into an emulator program like Calibre to see how it will look on the Readers it will be sent to. It may not be precisely WYSIWYG, but it will be a lot closer than what you see on your desktop or laptop in your editing package.

Uploading your file

Accept that every site you upload your book to will have a different set of instructions that must be followed to ensure your content is as WYSIWYG as possible. They will more than likely have a handbook to guide you through the process. Read it. Archive it for future reference. Print it out if necessary.

If you employ a third party to convert and upload for you, ensure that they have read it, too. Remember, it's *your* content, and no one has a greater stake in ensuring that it displays correctly than you. Never assume that just because you've paid for professional services that everything's been done properly. Ask for a *proof* (the master file that will be sent to the eBook distributor) before the file is uploaded. If you can afford it, view the title on the target Reader device once it's been uploaded.

Online revisions

After you upload your content, you may discover that something's wrong. Someone who's bought your book may let you know. Or worse – pointed out its flaws online! In any case, remember that one key advantage of eBooks over physical ones is the relative ease of amending them. So fix it. As soon as possible.

Online sites will have a means whereby you can resubmit a refined title. It may be offline for a few days while they swap it, but generally it's an automated process, so they won't charge you for resubmitting it. If you do get the suggested change from someone who bought your book, offer to send it to them as an email attachment if you have the eBook version on your computer. It's all about good customer relations, right?

The Pay-off

If every author and publisher followed these quality control steps, we would be publishing better quality material. Authors and publishers would save themselves time and expense, and fewer readers would complain about poor production standards in the eBooks they have bought.

There's a real danger that, with the relative ease of publishing eBooks, standards could fall. If customers find that eBooks are lower in quality than their physical counterparts, we could see a backlash against e-publishing and books in general. Reputations rise and fall based on first impressions, so you want to make the best one possible with your first eBook. We all have a role to play and a stake in maintaining quality control in this new marketplace.

6. KISS and eBook Design

KISS in the eBook environment has less to do with love than you might think. It means *Keep It Simple, Stupid* in other contexts, and that sentiment certainly applies to eBook design, too.

Many designers, publishers, authors and readers see books as aesthetic objects – creating a sense of pleasure just by their appearance. While certain eBook formats can retain the aesthetic dimension of their print version, most formats destined to display in default on most current Readers are geared more to functionality than good looks.

This is in part because building in aesthetic features can add to a file's waistline, making your file bigger to send, store and receive. eBook editing programs can lead you into a false sense of security by offering you an array of font choices and options for including images and even audio files. But as we learned in the chapter on quality control, what you see on your eBook editor's screen may not display the same in some Readers, unless you know how to build in your font choices into the file you first create. So, the best advice is DIY Designer beware!

eBook Readers Have a Mind of Their Own

It may help to look at the end of the food chain. What exactly can most Readers display?

They're very good at displaying unbroken text. They flinch a bit at forced line breaks (to start a new paragraph), and a bit more at forced page breaks, but, thanks to the coding of content that happens in the background by eBook editing packages, they've learned to meet you halfway.

eBook Readers have a harder time with forced line breaks that start another line. A good example is poetry, which sometimes has very short lines. Unprocessed poetry in an eBook Reader or eBook editor is not a pretty sight. What you get is what the Reader is used to and therefore prefers: unbroken text, from left to right margin. That may include the title, and footnotes if any (prose authors, take note).

Once you've already imported your text into the eBook editor, there's no easy fix for missing line breaks. Most editing programs will require you to put in manual line breaks to separate the title from the body of the poem and an additional forced break between stanzas. Very time consuming. You'll wonder if you can be bothered.

Be economical with these manual breaks because, if you have too many in the wrong place, the Reader may decide to create an extra *page* break for you, which doesn't look good at all.

Font Choices, and Other Surprises

Fonts, too, can be a problem. The vast array available to you in programs like Word, InDesign and Acrobat are embraced by conventional and digital printing processes but not by most eBook Readers, if you simply import them without special processing. You may work from a master with all the design bells and whistles, but it will likely end up looking much more pedestrian on the Reader.

You can do two things here. Archive your master in the hope that sooner rather than later most Readers will be more sophisticated in what they can handle and behave as you wish. Or you can redesign your master to use *more* font choices, especially web-friendly ones like Helvetica, Arial, Geneva, Times New Roman and Verdana.

Font size can be an issue, too. Although Readers generally support characteristics like italics, bold and underline, they have problems with larger fonts, especially when those are set up in the original file with large 'leading' (the space between one line and the next). More often than not, the Reader sees larger fonts as too hard to deal with and simply breaks to a new page. Not good if your text is intended to start on the same page.

I suggest a maximum font size of 16pt for titles and chapter headings, working your way down the hierarchy from there. Both 14pt or 12pt are manageable for headings when you have 11pt or 10pt body text. Remember that most Readers allow the viewer to change the default display size, so your scheme can generally be enlarged to suit the viewer's preferences.

Body text from prose may simply 'reflow' in the Reader's screen, but this can still cause problems for poetry with long lines. Special coding is required to handle the indentation of following lines when a long line of poetry breaks. Poets would be well-advised to look critically at any poems with long lines, to consider how they will look if the text has to wrap to the following lines. This is especially necessary when the poet composes for A4 or letter page size and sees it as a divine right to use every character space between the left and right margins.

Graphics and photos can also be a challenge to lay out in the eBook environment. Both of these elements will be *referenced* by a good desktop publishing program. That is, the image is stored in an accompanying graphics file for embedding when the final eBook text file is prepared. In the case of xhtml files destined for the Kindle, the graphics file is generally stored as a compressed zip package.

An Ounce of Prevention

The key here is to try to do as much formatting as you can for your eBook *before* you get to the eBook editing stage—that is, when you are word processing the file in Word or Pages or laying it out in InDesign or Quark Xpress (don't even *think* of desktopping your file in a less sophisticated program.)

Now, what follows is not intended to be a detailed guide on how to use a word processing or desktop publishing packages. If you're not fluent with them, you probably shouldn't be attempting to convert your files to ePub or xhtml. That said, here are some important strategies to follow. Let's start with your text and its layout on the page.

1. Always format your content with Styles rather than using the tab or the dreaded space bar.
2. Assign *paragraph styles* to whole paragraphs.
3. Assign *character styles* to individual words within a paragraph that you want to look different from the rest of the paragraph, e.g. an italicised word should have an 'italics' character style attached to it.
4. If you want extra space between lines, stanzas or heading and text, control this through the 'space before' or 'space after' function in paragraph styles, rather than putting in a hard return. (As I mentioned earlier, ePub and other html based formats may ignore any formatting that is not attached to a style.)

Formatting Body Text

Your typical chapter in a prose book will start with a chapter title, then a first paragraph (the first line of which will not be indented) followed by body paragraphs that are indented. Each of these pieces of text will require-at minimum-their own *paragraph style* that sets the font, the font size and style, the justification, the amount of indentation from the left margin, the leading (space between lines) and any extra space before and after the paragraph.

When you reach the last paragraph in a scene and want to put in a line break, define this with a new style such as *Body Text Space After* where you build in a space after of something like 3mm or 12pt. These are directions that can be embedded in the file that will be exported to ePub or xhtml eventually, saving you work at that later stage, when it's more difficult to refine the coding.

Poetry that uses special indentations or a myriad of fonts can be a real challenge for eBook formatting. Each instance of indentation requires its own paragraph style, which you'll have to apply manually as you lay out the Word or InDesign file. Special fonts or font characteristics such as bolding, italics, and sub- or superscripts are controlled either by special *character styles,* if the word or phrase occurs in a line of normal body font, or by a paragraph style if the whole line is in the special font.

Formatting Master Elements

Master items are another element that require special handling at the word processing or desktop layout stage when you're preparing files for conversion to ePub or mobi.

Check your Word file for *anything* that appears in a header or footer (the recurring elements at the top and bottom of your pages), and delete it. The problem here is that the ePub *does* accept text in headers and footers, but it reproduces it in places you don't want it. So a running header may appear in the middle of a screen on one Reader or two-thirds of the way down the screen of another. If it's a page number, it won't make any sense at all because physical page numbers do not relate to screen views, nor do they automatically change between devices.

If you work in InDesign or Quark, where elements can be controlled on Master Pages, check to ensure you've deleted all textual elements, including page numbers.

This will save you time later on.

If you have elements like footnotes, indexes, appendices, etc., these can all be accommodated in your eBooks, but you may need to create special paragraph and character styles to distinguish them from your body text. For footnotes, you can use Word, Pages, or InDesign's automatic footnote features, or you can format them manually. Remember, though, that any footnote numbers will need to be coded to a special superscript character style; otherwise ePub will see them as regular numbers, rather than superscripts.

Tables of Content

And then we have Tables of Content (TOC). (You may want to call them Tables of Discontent after you see what needs to be done to handle them!) Desktop programs are good at setting out your TOC automatically, if you have set up your chapter titles properly by attaching them to a special paragraph style, something original like 'Chapter Head'. The program will dutifully scan your file for all instances of 'Chapter Head' and then compile your TOC, complete with page numbers—voilá!

The problem is that those page numbers will be irrelevant and downright misleading in an ePub file. So strip out ALL page numbers from your TOC, but retain the headings themselves. InDesign CS6 offers you the ability to link your headings in the TOC with the proper place in the file using hyperlinks. Word and Pages do this as well, but I'd be less trusting of the results. The coding may or may not go with the file when it's exported to ePub or xhtml, so it's best to set up your hyperlinks in InDesign, or at least double-check the links once you transfer from your word processing file into InDesign.

Here's how you double-check the links in InDesign:

1. Access the *Hyperlinks* editor in InDesign by going to Window/Interactive/Hyperlinks.
2. Place an insertion point in front of the text you want to link *to,* i.e. your chapter title.

3. Assign an *anchor* to this point by asking InDesign to create a new *hyperlink destination.* Note down the anchor number.
4. Do this for all the chapters in the file.
5. Back in your TOC, select the TOC heading, return to the Hyperlinks window and select *hyperlink destination options.*
6. Scroll down to find the appropriate anchor number (did you remember to copy it down?) and click OK.
7. Do this for each element in your TOC.

Graphics, Pictures and Tables

If you haven't given up by now and decided to outsource the design of your file to someone in India, the last thing you have to consider is any graphics or photos that you want in your eBook. The good news is that ePub and xhtml allow such elements to be included in the file. But most consumer level editing programs do not allow for the wrapping of text around these elements in basic ePub and xhtml files, at least at the time of this 2nd edition.

This is a good time to consider *optimizing* your elements. While photo size may be a trivial concern with a print file, it can be a major concern in an eBook. If you've done any webpage design, the principle here is the same: if it's a graphic, it needs to be optimized for screen viewing. My program of choice for this is Photoshop CS6, but recent versions of Photoshop will do, as will Adobe's web-oriented Fireworks program.

With your photo open in Photoshop, go to *File > Save for Web,* which will open the image in a web editing window. Generally High Resolution (60% quality) will work fine on screen, except if you need small detail rendered as well as possible. In this case you could lift it up to 80% or even 100% and still have considerable space saving via Photoshop's automatic compression function, although 60% is almost always sufficient. You then have the option of selecting the image file format. Jpeg or png will work fine.

As you optimize, save each image into a special Images folder that you'll be able to access as you work on the file in your ePub or xhtml editing program.

Remember those color images you had to convert to grayscale to save physical printing costs? The good news is that eBook Readers don't charge any more for people to view in color or grayscale, so by all means substitute your color images back into your eBook files.

Want to ensure that your graphics stay with the text they're intended to be seen with? If you've got InDesign 5.5 or 6, look for the *Articles* function under the Windows menu at the top. Opening this will bring up a control panel that allows you to define elements on particular pages simply by selecting them with your cursor and then clicking the (+) button in the

Articles panel. When you export, if you've done it properly, your graphics and text will appear in the proper sequence in the exported file.

Exporting for ePub

Once you've done all the above, and ensured that someone has double-checked your work, it's time to export the file for ePub production. There are online options out there for doing this, but I've found that a good program for this purpose is ***Sigil.*** It's free to download, is cross-platform, and it has most of the features you want in an ePub editor. So, for the sake of brevity, it's the only ePub editor I'll be talking about in this Kit.

You'll first need to export the file from InDesign to create the ePub file. But before you do this, you should complete some metadata information on the InDesign file itself. With the file open on your desktop, go to *File > File Info.* This will bring up a window with fields to complete about your file, including the crucial ones: Title, Author, Description, Keywords and Copyright Notice. If you complete these fields now, they will export into ePub along with the text as hidden content, saving you work at the ePub editing stage.

Next, you can export the file itself. *Go to File/Export for ...* and then select the ePub option. A window will come up asking you for more information on how you want the file to be handled. Three general fields will appear: General, Images, Contents. For *General,* identify the Publisher; the ISBN as the Unique

Identifier; and select View eBook after Exporting to save yourself a click or two. For *Images,* usually you can leave the fields as is unless you particularly want a higher resolution applied to your images and graphics. You'll probably be importing optimized images from the folder we set up above anyway, so you can probably leave the fields as is. For *Contents,* the only thing you need to do is select Include InDesign TOC entries, which will activate the hyperlinks you set up earlier.

Once that's all done, click Export and let InDesign do its job.

Working with Sigil

Sigil looks very much like a stripped down html editor, which it is, except that it's designed to work on ePub files. Here's the way the process works.

Once the program has opened your ePub file, you'll see a series of folders in the vertical bar on the left: *Text, Styles, Images, Fonts* and *Misc.* Only the top three will be of any importance to us.

In the main window will be your document in one continuous file, without any page breaks. Any graphics you weren't able to code with the Articles panel (see Graphics, Pictures, Tables section) will probably have shifted to the end of the file, along with other blocks like footnotes and indexes that the export feature couldn't keep with the main document.

Your first job will be to put in the necessary page breaks. Sigil and ePub don't know where you want the pages to break, but if you don't tell them they'll put them in for you in the strangest of places. Better to define them here than leave it to chance.

First, click an insertion point where you want the page to break, no matter what Reader is viewing it. Then find the *Split at Cursor* icon in the top menu bar. It's just to the left of the icon that looks like a screen. Click on it, and voilá, you have a page break. In the left vertical bar, a new xhtml icon will appear with a generic number. You can retitle this by right-clicking on it and selecting *rename,* but keep any new label simple and probably to one word, e.g. 'Cover' or 'Chap1'.

Go through the entire file, inserting page (chapter) breaks where you need them. This has the effect of creating new xhtml files with each split you've made.

You'll then want to review the text itself. Sometimes, especially if you have left or full justification on, the ePub file will do its best to properly word-wrap the lines, but it may not do this perfectly.

You may find lines with huge spaces between words. There is a way of fixing these in Sigil, even though they may reproduce OK in the Readers without modification here. The trick I use is to copy a character space between the full stop at the end of one sentence and the first letter of the next, copy it, then paste it in before the start of a new sentence in the troubling line. That will generally solve the problem.

The export sometimes may seem to lose text for no reason. Watch for an odd space between lines with what appears to be a gap in the text. If you place your cursor in front of the word that continues after the missing text and then back-space, the missing text will reappear, as if by magic! Again, pasting in an extra character space should fix the problem.

Sigil does offer some default font (paragraph) styles in a drop-down menu that starts with Normal, but avoid invoking these at all costs. They will invariably conflict with any styles you've exported from InDesign. If you find there is a paragraph or character formatting problem, you'll just have to go back to InDesign to fix it and then export again. Unless you know enough to modify the CSS code in Sigil. Yes, I know ... *groan.*

Interestingly, you are able to cut and paste blocks of text within the ePub file while editing in Sigil, and you may even be able to cut and paste text in from the InDesign file, but I don't recommend doing this. Even though it may look fine in Sigil, it almost certainly will not look as you intended in the Reader.

If you kept images in your InDesign file before exporting the file rather than using the Articles panel I mentioned earlier, they will generally end up at the end of your ePub file, waiting for you to insert them in their proper place. You'll find them listed by name in the Images folder in Sigil. If you went to the trouble of optimizing your images in Photoshop and then relinked to them in InDesign, most of your work will be done. It's just a matter of cutting and pasting in the images where they're needed.

If you simply created a new folder for your optimized images, you'll have to paste them into the ePub file using the top menu Images icon, which is just to the right of the Split at Cursor icon. Keep in mind, though, that once you've put the images in, you'll need to delete the originals from the Images folder by right clicking on each image and selecting Remove as the option. Unfortunately, Sigil doesn't allow you to select and delete several images at once.

Once everything looks as it should, it's time to *validate* the file.

epubcheck is a free testing application, currently in Version 3 for Mac and Windows, that I highly recommend. After installing the app on your hard drive, open it and then navigate to your ePub file. If the app finds any problems, it will list them for you, with a niggling "Bother!" at the end of the message. No news is definitely good news in this process.

If epubcheck identifies problems, you need to fix them. Otherwise, your eBook distributor will knock them back – unless they're careless.

Sigil also offers its own validator and a code view where, if you know something about editing html, you may be able to fix problems without having to go back to your InDesign master. epubcheck gives you just enough information on the error for you to locate it in Sigil's code view. However, if you create a clean InDesign file in the first place, include the necessary metadata and then export it as instructed, you should get the all-clear. Fingers crossed!

Testing in an Emulator or a Reader

Just because epubcheck gives you the thumbs up is no reason to break out the champers—yet. It only means that you have a valid ePub file that can be viewed on most generic Readers. It does not guarantee that it will display the file exactly as you intend it to look.

It's a good idea to view your validated file in an emulator program such as Calibre. Calibre offers the ability to view your file not only in ePub but also in other formats, as it will be seen on a variety of Readers. It also offers you a place to archive your books and to convert them for upload to your own device. It's promoted as an editing program as well, but we have found it to be less user-friendly than Sigil at fixing defective ePub files. If you can't fix the code in Sigil you might have to go back to your InDesign master.

Handling Images in ePub

IP converts a number of picture books to ePub. These raise a special challenge, even after they pass epubcheck. Most of these books have pages that are intended to display as two-page spreads. For a Reader, this essentially means viewing in landscape format. With some of the more advanced devices like the iPad that are capable of displaying books in landscape as well as portrait format, this is not a problem. But for basic reading software such as ***Adobe Digital Editions*** (ADE), the page will display as portrait, so we're doomed if we don't modify the two-page spreads before exporting to ePub. Without special coding, at least 40% of the image will be cut off from the ADE viewer window if the Reader has a small screen. It will be OK on larger screens where the viewer has the ability of expanding the ADE window.

You may never experience this problem if you don't have to export pages containing text that you want to keep with images, as is the case in picture books. As I've already said, without the coding from the Articles panel of InDesign, the ePub will send text one direction and images in the other when exporting. This means that the text you have in your typical picture book, which is layered on top of the image, will not stay there.

To deal with this issue, we used to export picture book pages from InDesign as image files (similar to what you do for images) and then place them separately within the Sigil ePub file. Sigil accepts them, and epubcheck passes them. But when they are viewed on a basic Reader such as ADE, the viewer window still had to be resized to accommodate them. Further, Apple will probably reject the file for the iBookstore because the text-now being a part of the image-is not searchable.

For those of you game to keep Apple happy and to do a bit of special coding for these spread oriented files, skip to the next section, Fixed Layout ePubs.

Keep in mind that, without special coding, you will likely have to resize your images anyway for ePub conversion. Standard print size images are far too big. And even though ePub Readers may be able to resize the image automatically, it will take up too much space, and many of the distributors will reject the file outright. Generally, the maximum size you want for a full page portrait image is 600 pixels wide x 800 pixels high. Downsize from there for images that are to appear smaller in relation to the accompanying text.

Another limitation of earlier versions of ePub was its inability to wrap text around your images. This meant that you couldn't have text to the left or right of your image, unless you'd exported the image and the text together as a image file. You'd have to consider how this limitation affects the design and layout of the file as it will appear on most Readers.

So, what we've had to do is to create a special ePub file that can be used by basic emulation software such as ADE and maintain the full sized file for the more advanced Readers. Forewarned is forearmed!

And Then There Was Fixed Layout

Something had to give in page layout in eBooks. Publishers of kids books, graphic novels, cookbooks and some academic titles were pulling their hair out – if they hadn't already shaved their heads by then.

So the ePub people decided to put their shoulder to the wheel and develop some code conventions that would allow designers to place elements on the page precisely and to add text over images, or even images over other images. The way this is done is in the code, either on the xhtml pages themselves or behind the scenes in the CSS styles. The page dimensions, especially height and width, are defined in pixels. Then, every element on the page is positioned precisely on the page in relation to the layer it lives on and its distance from the top and the left side of the page.

This can be complicated stuff, and is certainly not for the faint-hearted, but, if you believe that being well informed is better than staying in the dark and being fed mushrooms by eBook converters, read the key elements that distinguish a Fixed Layout (flePub) file from a normal ePub:

- The page dimensions are set in *spreads* rather than pages and controlled by *meta content* code with a *viewport* of a fixed height in pixels, described in code as follows:

```
<html xmlns="http://www.w3.org/1999/xhtml">
<head>
<metacontent="width=626, height=820"
 name="viewport"/>
```

- Each font in the document must be defined by the CSS according to point size and characteristic, so an italics font must have its own CSS code unique from the regular version of that font, e.g.:

```
@font-face {
font-family: "HoboStd";
font-style: normal;
font-weight: normal;
src: url(../Fonts/HoboStd.otf);
```

- All elements, including text, are positioned on defined *layers* defined within *div* codes (divisions, essentially paragraphs in plain-speak). Text blocks can be on the same layer, so long as they are not expected to overlap (overprint), e.g.:

```
div.sgc-6 {position:abso-
 lute;left:312px;top:742px;}
div.sgc-5 {position:abso-
 lute;left:285px;top:640px;}
div.sgc-4 {position:abso-
 lute;left:285px;top:620px;}
div.sgc-3{position:absolute;left:88px;top:112px;}
div.sgc-2{position:absolute;left:88px;top:82px;}
```

```
div.sgc-1{position:absolute;left:88px;top:62px;}
/*]]>*/
</style>
```

Each line of div code corresponds to a paragraph block of text, showing its distance from the left side and top of the page, respectively. Each paragraph then is listed separately, e.g.:

```
<div class="ch sgc-1">
<span class="small">A</span>nd  when <span
 class="small">L</span>ily  and <span
 class="small">A</span>manda  got home they
 weren't happy
</div>

<div class="ch sgc-2">
and smiling and ready to help around the house.
</div>

<div class="ch sgc-3">
<span class="small">T</span>hey  were glum
 and gloomy and even a bit lazy.
</div>
```

...and so forth. Got that?

The flePub has a couple of other important elements to make it work correctly:

- Separate *xhtml files* corresponding to chapters of the document.

- Separate folders containing your *images, fonts* and *styles* (the CSS variety).
- The *content.opf,* which begins with *metadata* (key words describing what's in the file) and then every element in the document and its source, e.g.:

```
<?xml version="1.0" encoding="utf-8" stan-
dalone="yes"?>
<package xmlns="http://www.idpf.org/2007/o
pf" uniqueidentifier="bookid" version="2.0">
<metadata xmlns="http://www.idpf.org/2007/
opf" xmlns:dc="http://purl.org/dc/elements/1.
1/">
<dc:title>The Giggle Gum Tree</dc:title>
<dc:creator>Juliet Williams Elizabeth Bot-
té</dc:creator>
<dc:date>2012-07-11</dc:date>
<dc:identifier
id="bookid">9781921869532</dc:identifier>
<dc:language>en</dc:language>
<meta content="cover-image" name="cover"/>
</metadata>
<manifest>
<item href="toc.ncx" id="ncx" media-
type="application/x-dtbncx+xml"/>
<item href="Styles/stylesheet.css" id="css"
media-type="text/css"/>
<item href="Styles/stylesheet1.css" id="css1"
media-type="text/css"/>
```

```
<item href="Fonts/AGaramondPro-Regular.otf"
 id="font-1" mediatype="application/x-font-
 ttf"/>
<item href="Fonts/HoboStd.otf" id="font-2"
 media-type="application/x-font-ttf"/>
<item href="Fonts/Skia.ttf" id="font-3" media-
 type="application/x-font-ttf"/>
<item href="Fonts/Papyrus.ttf" id="font-4"
 media-type="application/x-font-ttf"/>
<item href="Fonts/LetterGothicStd.ttf"
 id="font-5" media-type="application/x-font-
 ttf"/>
<item href="Fonts/LetterGothicStd-Bold.ttf"
 id="font-6" media-type="application/x-font-
 ttf"/>
<item href="Text/page_001.xhtml" id="pg001"
 media-type="application/xhtml+xml"/>
<item href="Text/page_002.xhtml" id="pg002"
 media-type="application/xhtml+xml"/>
```

- The *toc.ncx* (a coded Table of Contents), which lists each chapter (xhtml file) in the proper order.

Before you reach for the Yellow Pages to look up Outsourcing, let me add that a properly formatted InDesign file will give you most of what you need as the basis for an ePub file. You then need to apply the specific code to define each spread and where the elements will be positioned.

However, nothing is as simple in the eBook world as it could be if the big distributors could just agree on a standard for formatting files, and Fixed Layout is no different. There's a generic flePub that will work on most devices for most things, and then there's a special Kindle Fixed Layout format (KF8) that works only on Kindle devices. Why? Because Amazon want it their own way, of course!

Can you format Fixed Layout files on your own, with a minimum amount of knowledge of coding? Probably not. And, if you're brave enough to want to try, you will almost certainly need a handbook that trots out the nitty gritty of flePub coding for you.

However, you can get your hands dirty if you download some titles from Apple or Amazon and then deconstruct them. That is, open them up in Sigil or Calibre, and look at the CSS and xhtml code that creates the kind of effect you want on particular pages and try to replicate or adapt that for your project.

Striking a Match under Kindle

For most of you, flowing eBooks will be all that you need, so let's look at what Amazon requires for these.

Amazon prefer the .mobi format, which is essentially xhtml—a bit closer in nature to what is used for web pages. While it's true that xhtml may be easier to handle for coding purposes, it is probably more limited in terms of its ability to handle enhanced content, especially since developers are investing more resources in upscaling ePub's functionality for handling multimedia.

That said, it's probably not a winning strategy for us to wait until Amazon decides to embrace ePub. You'll need to create a file that will work on the Kindles NOW.

If you've registered as a Kindle content provider, you'll find that Amazon accepts all sorts of formats for uploading, e.g. pdfs and even Word files. However, what comes out the other end may well disappoint you if you decide to shortcut the conversion process. Amazon has had a message up on their site for years promising to address the problems with their online conversion process. As yet, no improvements have surfaced.

If you send them a file other than an xhtml file, their online converter processes it, and then you get a message advising you to preview the results. You can be almost certain that it won't be exactly what you want, or even close to it. At that stage, you'll have to export the file into your favorite html editor, fix things and then upload the file again. Or, as I recommend, do your best to get it right *before* sending it to Amazon. What follows is, hopefully, a winning strategy, at least with the current state of play in mind.

Recently, Amazon released an offline converter/previewer for xhtml to .mobi called, strangely enough, *Kindle Previewer.* You download the application, feed it your xhtml files at your convenience, test, edit, refine and finally upload to Amazon – much easier than doing everything online.

But before we submit the file to Amazon, we need to get it ready for conversion.

Preparing the xhtml file in Dreamweaver

The good news is that you'll be able to use the same master for your xhtml file as you had for the export to ePub. From InDesign, open the file again, go to File/Export for ... but this time choose Dreamweaver, which is the html editor included in Adobe Creative Suite.

There are pluses and minuses with editing in Dreamweaver – or any advanced html packages. One advantage is your ability to create CSS (cascading style sheets) right in the program. Web editors offer you a limited selection of fonts, grouped within families, that are regarded as 'web friendly', that is, viewable as authored in a variety of browsers.

The downside – and a very big one – is that you can't override these web-friendly fonts with the more exotic ones you might have used in your InDesign files. Most browsers will simply default to the fonts available to them. This means that your Kindle version may well look less aesthetically pleasing than the ePub version.

Another disadvantage of working in xhtml for the Kindle is that you have little control over page breaks. The Kindle will flow your text into the available space, but where the page breaks fall will depend on the viewer's choice of display size, which is set on the Reader. You might gain some control by putting in extra hard returns to space out elements in the hope that the Reader will jump to a new screen when finding the blank space, but it's just as likely to create a blank screen, so this is not recommended.

But another plus of working in xhtml, and its more advanced cousin xml, is the ability to embed multimedia enhancements like audio and video. Flash and Quicktime are applications that can create compressed audio and video that can be included with a web page, although at this point in time the Kindle can only handle mp3 audio. ePub3 has the ability to incorporate multimedia, but you'll need to be adept at coding the elements in.

Formatting Styles in Dreamweaver

As mentioned above, most of the trouble you went to in formatting styles in Word/Pages/InDesign will largely be wasted when it comes to xhtml design and layout, except for providing you with an initial roadmap of how you wanted the file to look, at least in terms of its style hierarchy. You'll either have to use the CSS styles included with Dreamweaver or create your own more exotic ones. Keep in mind that there are no guarantees that the Kindle – or any other reading devices – will display your styles as you wish them to be viewed. Most eBook publishers prefer to take an optimistic stance on this by creating more advanced CSS styles in the hope that the newer devices will be able to handle them.

Where to once I have my ePub or xhtml file?

That's a topic I'll cover in greater detail later on, but generally your options are to either upload your file directly to a distributor, or to a packager, a company that uploads the file for you. The bigger distributors like Amazon and Apple prefer to deal with third parties who are more experienced with the required workflow. However, other distributors like ***Smashwords, Kobo,*** BookBaby, and Barnes & Noble (for the ***Nook***) will accept content directly from authors as well as publishers. But read the small print: packagers and publishers are sometimes able to negotiate better terms with these distributors than individuals can. You may end up with about the same royalty with a packager as you can get directly from the distributor and save yourself the work of uploading, proofing and accounting for sales. As always, read every contract BEFORE you sign!

For further information and resources for intermediate users on converting files, especially using CS software packages like InDesign and Dreamweaver, please check out Colleen Cunningham's article ***InDesign to eBook: Resources*** from Digital Book World.

iBooks Author

Recently, Apple, Inc released ***iBooks Author,*** a proprietary app that, in theory at least, makes ePub construction a breeze. The good news is that you don't have to write a line of code to author in iBooks Author, which means you don't need an ePub editor or even a validation program. You don't even need to look for a distributor for your eBook once it's complete: Apple iBookstore is literally just a click away.

The other neat thing about iBooks Author is all the free bells and whistles. You can add audio and video via widgets and place them anywhere (well, sort of anywhere) on the page. Indeed, you have considerable control over everything on the page, because back-stage, iBooks Author is a close cousin of ePub3, and therefore a lot more powerful in handling enhancements than ePub2.

That's the good news. But it's not all good. The biggest drawback to using iBooks Author is that the file you create will only work on Apple devices. You can't use it with Kobo or Barnes & Noble, or any of the other ePub distributors. That's because Apple has introduced their own special code that won't work on these other platforms. And even if it did, you've signed an agreement with Apple that says you're not allowed to sell it anywhere else, even directly from your own website.

Still want to sell to Amazon, Kobo, Barnes & Noble and the rest? You'll still have to create an ePub to work elsewhere, plus a .mobi for Amazon. Sound like more work? Yes, it is. But, if this is your first foray into eBooks and you will be content to send your masterpiece to just Apple and Amazon, it means less work for you. You'd have to create the .mobi file for Amazon, and Apple is happy to do their branded ePub version for you in iBooks Author.

Want to give it a try? Read on. Otherwise, off you go to Chapter 7, which is all about outsourcing, i.e. paying someone else to get their hands dirty with your book (conversion).

Before you get all excited about plunging into iBooks Author, if you don't have a Mac, you can stop reading this section now, since there is no PC version of the application as yet. Will Apple follow the iTunes route and create a PC version down the line? I really doubt it. iBooks Author is about marketshare, making Apple devices the platform of choice and discouraging people from selling their books elsewhere. One way of doing that is to discourage them from even creating their books outside of the Apple environment.

So, for those happy Mac users still with me, here's the process in a nutshell:

- Open iBooks Author.
- Choose a template that suits your title.
- Import a Pages or Word file; add graphics/pictures as needed using the Insert Menu.

- Arrange your text according to the iBooks Author hierarchy (Chapters, Sections, etc.).
- Add chapters (page breaks) where you need them.
- Drag in widgets to contain audio or video elements and caption them.
- Ensure that everything is coded according to paragraph and character styles. (No, iBooks Author doesn't do this for you automatically!)
- Ensure that everything that needs to be listed in your Table of Contents is.
- Proofread, save, Publish (send) to the iBooks Store (there's a big blue button on the menu bar for this!).

Now, wasn't that easy?

Some caveats and tips. iBooks Author was designed for neophytes, that is, people who are not designers or code-heads and do not wish to become such creatures. To make it easy for those people, iBooks Author presents you with Templates at the opening page, and you're expected to choose one for your book. Problem is, like all templates, they will either sort of work for your project or not really be suited for it at all.

Your choice here is to import other templates that are better suited to your project or start from scratch. If you google <iBooks Author free templates> or do a search on the Apple site, you'll find a range of extra templates that may be closer to the mark you need. Alternatively, you can start with one of the standard templates and strip it down to its bare essentials (Chapter pages and Section pages).

For those of you who have gone beyond a Pages or Word file to import, you can actually cut & paste in an InDesign file by spreads, in effect creating a flePub, which is very good news for the picture book authors among you, but not so good news for those who prefer to write 600 page sagas.

Apple is not completely the bad guy on the distribution side from iBooks Author. You *can* give away your iBooks Author file, or create a pdf from it, also to give away. How does Apple plan to police this process to restrict you from then selling the pdf? Perhaps, when you install the program, it implants a cookie deep in your hard drive that reports back to an Apple Genius about any infringements. I don't know; and I have no plans to test this.

7. Does one size fit all?

After reading (& perhaps re-reading?) the previous chapter, you may be feeling less than confident about converting your first book to eBook format. It's always harder the first time, and you *will* make mistakes, but you will *learn* from those mistakes and do better with each new title you convert.

But what do you do if you have only one book to convert and no plans to write any more? Is it worth the angst, even with your faithful Kit by your side? You may decide to hire someone to do it for you with the expectation it will go more quickly and flawlessly. What are 'experts' for, after all?

But finding a reputable converter is easier said than done, and this is certainly *buyer beware* country. There are no university degrees in eBook production – yet. And there's no prohibition against people advertising themselves as 'experts' in the field and charging you top fees.

So how can you tell if you're dealing with an 'expert' rather than a spin artist? Ask the right questions!

But before you do that, you need to learn what those questions are.

An Expert Should Have a Track Record

You may have come across their name via an internet search, and now you're browsing their website. What do you look for?

An expert should, of course, have put up a number of runs on the board before advertising their services. The last thing you want is to pay by the hour for someone to use your precious material as work experience or a case study.

Consider their pitch. Do they go into detail about the projects they've worked on, or simply assert their areas of interest? An eBook is not a single church: there are as many eBook genres and sub-genres of writing. Technical books. Scientific books. Poetry. Educational texts. Fiction. Art books. Cook books. These projects are different in nature and are handled differently in the print environment, so you should expect they will have special requirements in eBook production as well.

So one of the first questions you should ask your shortlisted 'expert' is whether they have experience converting *your* kind of book. It's also worth asking what platforms they've sent content to. A Kindle expert may not be an iPad expert, and vice-versa.

Describe your project to them. Ask if they have any special requirements for your setting it out before you send it to them. If they simply say 'just send it in', you probably have reasons for concern.

Have a close look at your title. What design features are important to you? Make a list and ask the expert how they will ensure that the eBook version looks as close to how you visualise it as possible. If they're evasive or say something to the effect that they'll do the best they can, warning bells should sound.

As you'll have learned from previous chapters, eBook conversion does involve *some* compromises, but the applications are flexible enough to build in sufficient aesthetic features to allow your eBook version to at least resemble its print counterpart. Ask your expert what will be possible in design and what won't. The answers may be quite revealing.

Also ask them how they test the converted version before sending it to you or uploading it to a distributor. If they don't describe a workflow that involves validating each project with a program like epubcheck and then viewing the converted file in simulators like Calibre or on actual readers like the Kindle or Adobe Digital Editions, you may well be short-changed and end up having to edit your work if it fails validation. Do they send you the ePub or xhtml file so you can check it yourself before they upload it?

Testimonials

Consultants are fond of putting up testimonials on their website to convince you that they can do a fine job. It's only common sense to regard such inflated reviews with caution. When's the last time you read a negative testimonial or review on a website? Check the sources of the testimonial. Is the author someone you've heard of, or someone who works for a high profile company or agency? That might lend credibility to what has been said, but I certainly wouldn't entrust my work to an expert solely on the basis of testimonials.

Ask the expert what authors or publishers they've worked for and whether or not those clients would be willing to supply you with a reference. You might not bother to follow through with this, but if they come up empty-handed, that might tell you something about their ability to deliver for you.

The bigger online distributors like Apple, Overdrive and Amazon sometimes maintain lists of service providers who will work with you, for a fee. These leads may be worth checking out. Even if they charge a bit more than the going rate, they may well work more quickly and turn around a better product. Certain distributors like BookBaby and Smashwords provide you with a free guide to help you through the mine field. Some may even offer to upload your work to a range of retailers and wholesalers, which may be tempting, but read the small print. Ensure that you will still be listed as publisher and that all royalty payments will come directly to you.

One-Stop Shops

eBook conversion and distribution is a rapidly expanding industry and numerous companies are surfacing with offers to provide all or part of the services you require.

While I hesitate to recommend any of these to you, it might be worth having a look at companies like ***Aptara*** as a possible provider. IP at present does its own conversions through the Digital Publishing Centre (DPC), but we do contact Aptara and other companies as partners when we have too much work to handle. What I like about Aptara is that they provide newsletters and free webinars to keep their clients up-to-date on what's happening in the industry. This suggests to me that they're in it for the long run, wanting to establish relationships with their clients rather than just taking your money and running with it. And they also work for major publishers like Walker Books.

It might be a good starting point to use Aptara as a benchmark against which to compare other possible providers in level and detail of service as well as cost.

If you do decide to outsource, make it clear that you are inviting quotes from a number of providers. The industry is highly competitive as companies are seeking to establish their reputation, so you could well get a better price this way.

One-stop Conversion Shops

But what of the other companies who promise to do everything for you, including file conversion, uploading to online distributors, and collection of royalties and accounting?

Smashwords offers all of the above – and more. They'll even assign your work an ISBN at no charge – if you let them be listed as the work's publisher. The upside here is that you get a free ISBN, which can cost AU $40 if you order it through Thorpe in Australia, plus a one-off publisher registration fee of AU $55. And Smashwords distributes beyond their own site, giving you the option of having them upload to Amazon for the Kindle, Apple for the iPad/iPhone, and Barnes & Noble for the Nook.

The downside is that bibliographic entries will list Smashwords as the publisher in the bibliographic entries, not you, which suggests they are the only source for sales of the work. You could quickly lose far more in sales from your own website or blog than it would cost if you purchased your own ISBN and retained your status as the work's publisher. Also keep in mind that, if you decide to list the work with other distributors, they could baulk at doing so if they see a competitor as the publisher through the ISBN.

Other companies like ***Kobo*** go further than Smashwords in offering authors value for money. For a fee, they'll convert your work to ePub, list it on their site and even send you the ePub file, which you can later amend or distribute elsewhere. Listing with Kobo previously had the advantage of making your work available to the now liquidated Red Group Retail network (Pearson PLC in Australia, formerly Angus & Robertson; Whitcoulls in New Zealand; and Barnes & Noble internationally, formerly Borders). That was good coverage, which could complement your exposure on Amazon, if you send to the Kindle, or on iTunes, if you upload to Apple.

More recently on the scene is ***BookBaby.*** An offshoot of the indie music distributor CD Baby, BookBaby offers a flat service fee of US $99 for converting your file to ePub and .mobi for its major online store. Through *Hostbaby,* you can also create your own basic website. There's an annual archiving fee of US $19 per title, but otherwise, BookBaby does all the distribution and accounting for you and takes 0% of the net revenue.

From all reports, they have good customer service and reasonable quality control. But remember, unless you pay extra, they do not edit or proofread your work; that's still up to you.

Before you rush out to sign up with one-stop companies like these, be sure that they'll be able to convert your title to an acceptable ePub or xhtml version. With Kobo, you get the actual file they'll be selling on their site, so you can test it on ADE or your Reader and let them know straight away if there are any problems. But with Smashwords, you'll have to wait until the title becomes available on the Kindle or the iPad before you can test it. I'd certainly be monitoring the situation as closely as possible to ensure that, if there are problems, they can be fixed quickly – before too many people buy your eBook and decide to return it because it doesn't look professional.

What are the chances of getting it right the first time? Logic would dictate that the more hands-on the conversion process is, the greater the chance of picking up and sorting out any idiosyncrasies in your work. A 'muncher' device is largely automated, and geared to converting blocks of prose text with few variants on conventional print presentation. The more your work departs from a straight prose book, the more likely it is that problems will arise, and the more on guard you'll have to be to ensure that the work is refined as quickly as possible once it goes on sale.

DIY as the Safest Option?

The biggest advantage of doing the conversion and uploading yourself is that you maintain control of the appearance of your work *before* it goes public. You export it from InDesign. You edit it in Sigil. You test it in epubcheck, on Calibre and in ADE before it gets uploaded. This means the work will be as good as it can be *before* someone buys it.

The next best approach is to find a trusted service provider who will do it for you manually, and guarantee that the essential steps are followed without fail. But, as I've said numerous times already, the buck stops with you. You should still be involved in the final testing and checking of your work before it goes live, or as quickly as possible after it's out there. Don't be afraid to spot mistakes. The sooner you correct them and re-send the file to the distributors, the less likely you'll be to get bad reviews from your readers.

8. What about the cost?

First, let's begin with a brief overview of the costs of preparing a physical book for pre-press, printing and distribution. This will help you compare the relative costs here with what you will face when you go digital, either yourself or with the help of a pro.

If we assume that authors are switched on enough these days to provide publishers with manuscripts in digital form to start with, rather than hard copy that has to be keyed in, or photographed/scanned before it can be laid out, the digital and physical pathways start very much on a level playing field. It really doesn't matter, at the editing stage, which channel the book is destined for. The amount of work require to lift it to publishable standard will likely be the same.

Some authors decide to short-circuit the editorial cycle by opting for 'instant' publication via vanity press. I certainly advise against vanity publishing, no matter how tempting it might be to get your work out there as quickly as possible. Speed doesn't breed success. We've already discussed the many reasons why authors should still rely on specialist readers and editors *before* publishing. Assuming that they do, the editorial costs will be much the same to this point.

Pre-production Costs

It is, of course, hard to estimate the cost of editing a book sight-unseen. Some would-be authors will ask editors for a blind quote, and we get enquiries like this all the time at IP, but this is very much a 'piece of string' question. How long is a piece of string? It is twice as long as it is from one end to the middle. How long will it take to edit a book? It will take as long as it takes.

Some editors will demand an hourly rate of $40-$80/hour and then estimate the number of days required to produce a polished draft; others may quote a rate per page. Both figures will be misleading if the editor hasn't viewed the project in advance, since some work will be a cake-walk (easy!) to edit while others may take ages to improve to the necessary standard. You also need to consider the expertise of the editor you're thinking of employing. An experienced editor will ask for a higher rate, but s/he will likely work more quickly, or at least provide better suggestions for improving it to publishable standard.

If you're dealing with a company like IP that offers multi-channel publication from the same title, little additional editing time will be needed to adapt a master destined for print into one to be published in digital form. We're still dealing with the same words on the page, but we may have to do some things to ensure those words look as close to the print original as possible.

Conversion Costs

Moving from an InDesign master prepared for print to one headed for ePub or xhtml publication does take additional time on top of that already expended for the print master. (Unless you're prepared to take the risk of subjecting a pdf of your work to a 'muncher' converter that supposedly makes it suitable for any Reader out there.)

If you go the more professional route, initially the file must be exported to the ePub or xhtml format. Then it must be reviewed to ensure that it not only looks good in the eBook editorial package, but also will work on the various devices and screens it may be heading for. The export from InDesign takes only a minute or so, with InDesign doing all the work in the background, but from there it can get more complicated, even tricky. The more complex in design your title is, the longer it will take to ensure the layout will work properly in the eBook environment.

eBook conversion companies will quote you anywhere from US $0.15–$0.40 per A4 or letter page, per format you want, although they may discount the price if you order more than one format conversion at a time. The cheaper prices are for straight text conversions like novels or essays; the higher rates are for more complex works containing illustrations and graphics, although they generally won't charge extra if you have just a few of these enhancements.

Some companies like Kobo offer a flat fee for about the first 200 pages and then a per page fee after that. So you can pay between US $29–$120 for a 100-page book conversion to ePub, depending on who you're dealing with. And you could pay almost as much again, or even more, if you require conversion to more than one format or to Fixed Layout formats.

With the current state of play, as I've said in previous chapters, the key formats are .mobi for the Kindle and ePub for almost every other Reader, although some publishers go further to produce formats geared to particular Readers, e.g. the Palm PDAs. Before making the decision to convert to these dedicated formats, ask yourself how many sales you're likely to make to these platforms and whether the sales are likely to cover your conversion costs. Given that Amazon make about two-thirds of all eBook sales at present, I would certainly start with a .mobi file and branch out from there as your budget and/or patience allows.

Digital Distribution Costs

What happens next depends on who's uploading your book and to where.

If you're working with companies like Kobo or Smashwords that offer conversion as well as distribution, there's no charge for uploading your book, but they do take a distribution fee that can be up to 55% of the eBook's net revenue. Remember that net revenue is not the same as the recommended retail or cover price of the book; it's what's left over after the distributor subtracts all the costs involved in selling your book. So, if someone higher up the food chain takes 30-40% of the cover price of your book as their fee, the net revenue might be as little as 60% of the cover price, leaving you with 25-30% of the cover price after your distributor deducts their share of the revenue.

This is quite a common scenario with distributors like Amazon, and it is what makes BookBaby an attractive prospect. However, even with them, the maximum they can return to you is 100% of what they get paid by Amazon and Apple.

Given the range of eBook Readers out there and the different sizes of screens and functionality, it's generally a good idea to thoroughly test the title before it gets uploaded. This is where most of the quick and nasty conversion services may try to cut corners. Testing can be time consuming, so "close enough is generally good enough" for these companies. If their quality control is slack, you may end up having to send your file to a pro to fix it, which can add US $100-$200 or more per format to your costs, depending on how much needs to be refined. Or you might have to develop thick skin to shrug off complaints that come in from buyers of your eBook about how it doesn't live up to their expectations.

If your book contains graphics (pictures, charts and graphs), these may have to be processed separately so they will work properly on the eBook Reader. In the chapter on conversion, I talked about the need to optimize your graphics and then to export them into a special folder from which they can be placed in your master ePub or xhtml file. If you have Photoshop or Fireworks on your computer, you can do this yourself, but, if you have to get a pro to do it for you, expect to pay Studio rates for this work in addition to what you'll pay for dealing with the body text of the work.

The good news is, as we've already learned, there are *free* software conversion packages like Sigil and Calibre available to keep your costs down (if you're willing to learn how to use them). Unless your title is complicated, you should be able to do most of the conversion tasks yourself. But until you're experienced at it, you should perhaps build in a few hours of freelance support in your budget to refine the title for distribution.

Promotion Costs

The even better news is that once your master meets the specification of the distributor, generally the only costs you'll face for making your title available will be the fees the distributor retains from the sales revenue. As I said at the outset, there won't be storage costs, or freight, or insurance, or paper-chewing vermin to worry about. Your title will be up in cyberspace and available for purchase 24/7.

Ironically, the greater access you have to the market may involve other costs you hadn't anticipated. It's one thing to send complimentary copies off to literary magazines and newspapers nationally in the hope of securing reviews that will prompt more buyers into the bookshops looking for your book. But how will you get it noticed internationally if you are unknown?

If you're content with letting the world beat a path to your door, there are probably little additional costs in sitting back to wait. However, most titles won't get noticed without an active promotional campaign. This is where your website, your blog and your social networking sites come into play.

Writing a blog and plugging into social networking sites are both free. Having a dedicated website may not be, if there is a cost in creating and maintaining it, along with the cost of establishing a specific domain (yourname.com). The other costs involved here may be in the fine-tuning of your website design and content if you're inexperienced at it, and perhaps costs for advertising in apps like Google Ads to try to more directly target your market. There is debate about the effectiveness of Google and Facebook ads, and other paid-for online campaigns. Quite a few people and companies use them, so they could be of benefit—if your title has sufficient universal appeal.

If your budget is tight, and you have free time to invest, you can still actively promote the title online. Facebook, Twitter and LinkedIn are prime social networking sites. Blogging sites like WordPress and Goodreads are an effective tool for developing a more detailed conversation with your audience. Also look for sites and online communities that share an interest with you. For example, if your book features horses, join an online equestrian club and talk about your book there! Find a way to promote your work via features you write, or contributions you make to online chats.

Some people recommend *online tours* as a way of raising your book's profile. Again, the only cost here is your time: finding online sites that would be willing to display a feature that you've written, or an interview with you as author commenting on issues relevant to the external online group. Like physical tours, the online tour generally is completed within a week and can be pretty exhausting while it's under way, but at least you don't have to worry about air fares and accommodation! If you can't set up a online tour to run for a week, you may still be able to convince other sites and blogs to feature plugs for your work, which is the next best thing. And this is something you'll want to do in any case once the online tour has finished.

It may be tempting to use eBook publication to 'test the market' before launching into physical publication if the title takes off, but keep in mind that you should carefully archive every master that's created along the way in case it is needed later on. Always prepare and save your masters at the highest resolution possible, as it's much easier to optimize a big master than it is to go the other way. Archiving everything, and then backing up your masters, is an essential part of your workflow. Nothing adds to the cost of publication or to your potential for migraine more than having to redo something that's already been done and lost!

Some people offer their titles for free or for drastically discounted prices for a limited time, on Amazon or via Goodreads competitions and elsewhere, in the hope of creating word of mouth. This strategy most certainly works better for genre titles such as romance than it does for poetry. But even if sales don't take off after you raise your price, you may have a warm glow knowing that a herd of people downloaded your book and are now hopefully enjoying it.

In summary, then, although you may face similar costs in getting your eBook ready for uploading as you would for conventional printing, generally your costs *thereafter* are minimal. The exception would be if you decided to mount a real world promotional campaign that included sending out samples of the book to international reviewers, or touring overseas.

Going digital still costs money, but the costs involved are different than that for convention publication. These costs may come down somewhat if and when the companies producing Readers agree on a single format, but until all devices handle files exactly the same, there will be significant costs involved in making sure your precious work displays as you intended wherever it's read.

9. Once you publish an eBook, you just sit back and wait for the royalties to roll in, right?

For years I've been offering a day-long workshop entitled *Selling That Book!* The workshop is very popular, and I've been invited back to several places to offer it more than once. People are curious about finding the magic formula (tricks of the trade?) that will make their book sell, even if they're being published by a major publisher.

There are several key principles to keep in mind, and most of them also apply to making your eBook successful. So let's start first with the common ground.

What works for physical and digital Books

It's easier to publish a book than to sell it. Most people with a decent computer and recent software have the tools necessary to make a physical book. And, as we learned in earlier chapters, they can also make an eBook with slightly more difficulty. Sometimes the process of making the book is so exhausting that we find it hard to follow through with the effort needed to promote it. But follow through we must!

The success or failure of a book may have less to do with its quality than your strategy for making your potential audience aware of it. It's been estimated that booksellers in Australia are confronted with 10,000 NEW titles per month. Booksellers in North America and the UK are certainly bombarded with even more than that. Quality is important. The appearance of the book is important, too. But if you don't know how to bring it to the booksellers' attention, it won't matter how good it is or how good it looks.

Professionals like editors, designers, promoters, reviewers and distributors have crucial roles to play in the success of your book. On the quality side, let me reiterate the importance of securing professional help and advice from either your publisher or freelancers you may hire to assist your self-publication. What's inside the covers may be less crucial in the first instance than the appearance of your book, but it will help when it comes to word-of-mouth promotion – still the most effective means of spreading the word.

Don't rush into choosing the title of your book. Reflect on it. Do your market research. Choose a title that's distinctive but not too esoteric. Something that's easy to remember and pass on between prospective readers.

If you're lucky enough to have an agent, or a publisher who's willing to invest resources on promoting your book, listen to the professional advice they offer you. Generally, it comes from years of experience and trial and error. They may not get it right every time, but they probably do pretty well at it.

Be realistic about your book's chances of becoming a bestseller. Poetry books, local histories and memoirs generally have a limited audience. Unless your book can win a major literary prize or attract media attention, the chances are it will sell only modestly, no matter how hard you try to promote it, and despite its inherent brilliance. Do what you can for small change or, better yet, for free.

Never miss a chance to remind the marketplace of the existence of your book and how to buy it. If your book is as good as your mother thinks it is, people will want to buy it as soon as it hits the shelves. Make sure it's easily available. The more steps (or clicks) a person has to go through to buy your book, the less likely they are to buy it.

Timing is crucial. The most successful books are generally right for the times. Often this is guess-work. If it weren't, more publishers (like yours truly!) would be driving a Mercedes.

Marketing a book is very much like marketing a product or a business. You need to have a plan. You need to stay in control and ensure that each crucial element in the Plan comes into play when it should. If you get major media coverage for your book two months before it becomes available, you've wasted your time, even though it may be good for your self-confidence. Most people will forget about your book within days or even hours of dramatic media exposure.

You also need to track sales very carefully. If you print 1000 copies in the first print run and sell 800 in the first month, by the end of the second week you should have told your printer to print another 1000, or maybe even 2000, as soon as possible. Again, you cannot expect your audience to wait weeks, or even *a* week, to get your book because it's out of stock and not available via POD. People are impatient. If they want something, they generally want it NOW.

Special Techniques for Digital Titles

OK. Most of this advice can be adopted or adapted without further explanation to eBooks, but are there other things you can do that are particularly suited to eBooks? Of course there are!

While marketing your book in the physical world is still important, you may find that your scarce resources are better invested in promoting activities in the environment where your book will live: in cyberspace.

I've already talked about some of the online strategies that you can adopt: creating and maintaining a website, blogs, social networks, online tours, etc. But maybe it's time to look at the fine print, the do's and don'ts of your online strategy.

Put yourself in the shoes of your potential buyers in designing and maintaining your online campaign. Don't assume that the same approach you use for your friends will work on people who don't know you or your work.

Most people will come to a commercial website only if they have a specific reason for doing so. Generally that will be to buy something they're after. But once they've found what they were after, will they come back? Not unless you make their first visit such a pleasant experience that they bookmark your page. Since so many commercial sites are, well, pretty ordinary, a well-designed website or blog has a better chance of staying in the viewer's mind.

You can also try to be informative as well as promotional. Explore the issues addressed in your book. Invite your viewers to join a chat, add their review – get engaged in a community of your readers. Add any external reviews and testimonials that come to your attention to your site.

If the book is geared at the schools, provide a teacher's guide so that adopting your book won't add to their workload if they're thinking of using it in class. (If you're not a teacher, get some help designing the guide from teachers, or maybe test the activities in the guide on groups of students).

Social Networking Techniques

Update your entire social networking profile several times per year. Provide useful links to complementary websites.

Add a slideshow if your book involves graphics or pictures. This isn't as hard as you might think. You can do it if you have a bit of knowledge of Flash, or even a presentation program like Keynote. Another option is to sign up to a commercial slideshow program like Smilebox (free!) that allows you to upload your slides to their server and then place a link to it on your website or blog or even Facebook/Twitter/LinkedIn.

For your blog: again, try to lift it a step above the personal. If people see that your blog is too self-serving, they won't come back to it. We don't need to know about your recent beach trip with your dog, but we do want to hear about your trips to the location of your novel.

Convey the sense that you're trying to create a community of shared interests, where you are a moderator or a resource person, rather than Big Daddy. Try to draw in other opinions, and encourage feedback. Pose controversial questions, and start the ball rolling with your own opinion on the issue. Encourage your visitors to pass on the word to their friends directly or via networks like Goodreads.

Try to avoid mixing business with pleasure. Set up a separate page for your book, and encourage people to follow you there. It's easier to control the tone of what's said on a business page, and readers are less likely to crack inappropriate jokes or divert the chat from the focus you want.

For your social networking sites (Facebook, LinkedIn, Twitter, etc.): use them exclusively to remind people about your book without pestering them about it. The key with social networking sites is to keep your name in front of your followers. This gentle approach may remind people who haven't yet bought your book to do so. They may also chat back to you about it, and in so doing, spread the word to their followers.

IP uses social networking sites to announce events and tours, and also to highlight reviews that have come in about our books. Nomination for prizes is also good news to put up, and followers generally take note of good news like that.

Encourage your followers to tag you and your book in their entries. And nothing is more motivating to your followers than a notification that you have tagged them on your book's Facebook page! They may well do some constructive tagging or liking in return. The more that happens, the more likely it will be that outsiders will be drawn to your site and join your community of interest.

Should you have a presence on *all* the key social networking sites? If you can afford the time, yes, but try to avoid repeating yourself between sites. It's better to have one excellent site than several so-so ones where you're spreading yourself too thinly. Some sites like Facebook offer you the option of replicating or at least excerpting your content on other sites like Twitter. This can work if you don't have the time to spend updating both sites, but it will tend to discourage people from following you on both – unless you also add special content now and then to the mirrored site. Also, if you duplicate posts from Twitter onto Facebook, the Facebook posts algorithm works actively against you, to make sure these posts never make it to the top of your fans' newsfeeds.

Word-of-mouth

Once you stake your claim to a slice of cyberspace, it's time to do some constructive colonising. Read what your viewers have to say on your pages; they may well point you to other groups and individuals who share a common interest.

Some of them may be VIPs like established authors and people with a high profile nationally, internationally, or in a community that you haven't visited before. Expand your list of social networking contacts.

And don't just simply accept new followers; write to them, saying something that suggests you've at least read their profile. Don't try to sell to them too quickly – work up to it.

Research

Do your online research, aside from the leads you might get from your social networking contacts. Look for general writing communities where you can discuss writing, get and receive feedback and talk about spin-off issues. Become familiar to others in the community, and then gently point them to your sites and encourage them to follow you.

Do a personal inventory on the subjects covered in your book, then communicate about them online. If what you have to say makes sense and is of value, you'll quickly become regarded as an authority or even a guru on it! Invitations to festivals and other events may well follow – and some of these may even be in the real world!

Ads

If you've spent much time online, you'll be aware of the opportunities you have to pay for advertising through Google, Yahoo, as well as the social networking sites like Facebook and LinkedIn. These sites make it easy to construct a small ad, and even assist you in tailoring it to your audience.

Google Ad campaigns can target general or specific audiences, but there is of course a cost, and there are never any guarantees that you'll recoup your investment. Generally, you're charged for 'click-throughs', where people click on your link from a website where your Google Ad has been placed. It doesn't matter if they go on to buy something from you; you're still charged for the exposure.

Facebook offers you the paid option of encouraging people to 'like' your page, but personally I find messages from people 'liking' their own page annoying, and I suspect many other people do, too.

Read the small print before you sign up for any such campaign. You may be able to set a weekly or monthly spend, and you may be offered a 'trial' or 'free time' with your ad. This is not unlike being offered $25 worth of free chips to gamble in a casino. The hope is that once you try the service, you'll stay with it. But, as with any such marketing campaign, you need to have a product that your audience is interested in buying. And your website or blog where they land as they click through needs to be geared to selling them the product with an attractive pitch.

If you have a bit of money to 'invest' in such campaigns, by all means give them a try, but keep in mind that it takes time to establish a profile, and you may have to spend a fair bit of money, with no immediate returns, to achieve that.

Book Trailers

Video promotion is another good way of spreading the word. Uploading to YouTube and Vimeo can be free, and you can develop a new fan base there by setting up your own channel to which people can subscribe.

But there's an art to creating a good book trailer, as there is in creating a film trailer. Putting up a bad one could be more harmful than not having one at all, so if you don't have the skills, call in the experts.

Video content can include readings and interviews, but try to keep it dynamic, rather than static Talking Heads. The ideal length is under three minutes, and every second of that should be engaging.

Youtube and Vimeo give you space to describe the work and meta-tag it, or even annotate or caption it.

It's workwhile doing this because it may attract more traffic to your trailer and thereafter to your store.

Freebies

If your advertising budget is tight or non-existent, there are plenty of ways to promote yourself and your book online, as discussed above. Amazon Author Central is a good place to establish yourself as a brand and point people to your titles.

On the social networking sites, keep your communications as personal as possible and place your work in front of your prospective buyer only after you've established a community of interest. They may be employing the same strategy on you, but that's what it's all about, isn't it?

10. Contracts and other legalities

Disclaimer:

As a publisher, I have some knowledge of contract and copyright law, but I do not pretend to be an expert. What follows will better inform you about the key issues in this area at this point in time, but you should rely on legal advice, and perhaps more than one legal opinion, where your actions could have serious financial implications.

Recently, Random House USA made the news by issuing a new children's book by *New York Times* bestselling author Michael Scott exclusively in digital format. It's about the death of Joan of Arc from his *Secrets of the Immortal Nicholas Flamel* series, which has sold more than a million copies in hard copy in the US to date. The eBook retails for US $0.99, a fraction of the cost of the physical prequels.

Will anyone make money out of this? With the growth of eBooks reported to be anywhere from 10-55% per annum of late, there is a chance that there will be some money in it, at least for Random House. Publishers still have the same pre-production costs whether they go physical or digital. And, as we have already learned, the costs of conversion to eBook versions like ePub, xhtml and xml can be substantial. After that, the major costs are marketing. The publisher has no printing, shipping or storage costs, and the costs of returns for eBooks will be minimal as the accounting can be done via automated systems that only require the occasional human oversight.

The Author as Content Creator

But what about the content creators? The most Michael Scott will make in royalties from his eBook would be something less than a dollar, and probably more in the range of 5-10 cents, if his contract with Random House were giving him the conventional 10% of the RRP. That's more than small change if you can sell a million copies of your book, but only if the sales volumes are high.

Chances are, though, that Scott's agent would have negotiated a rate much higher than the conventional print royalty. Royalty percentages of 25% of net revenue are fairly common on eBooks, with the percentage rising to 50% or more in some cases, especially for best-selling authors.

But before you use 50% as your goal in negotiations with your publisher, be aware that the higher percentages are usually for the spin-off eBook versions created after the existing print publications. Here, the publisher expects to have earned back all the production costs before the eBook is available. The print-book-first scenario is becoming less common of late.

More and more publishers are issuing eBook versions at the same time or even earlier than the physical version, even when the hard copy is to be released in hardback first. The risk for the publisher is that the physical book revenue will suffer as more and more people opt for the eBook version instead. So more eBooks will have to sell in the first instance for the publisher to cover costs, and this will invariably have a chilling effect on the level of royalty the publisher will be willing to offer.

Variable Royalties

In the short term, there are likely two scenarios for handling royalty levels. Option 1 would be a differentiated model, where the creators receive a lower percentage for the physical versions and a higher rate for the eBook versions, say 10% for the physical book and 25-50% for the eBook version. Option 2 would be an averaging model, where the publisher takes a punt and offers a figure of 20-25% based on the marketing department's projections of where the most sales are likely to occur.

Over the next few years, this is likely to be more guess-work than science, and this always makes financial people and lawyers a bit nervous. Which is why publishers like Faber & Faber's Stephen Page are calling for "flexibility" in contract provisions to allow for changes six months or a year into the life of a contract to ensure all parties are receiving a fair return.

Flexibility and fairness are fine in principle, but it still boils down to both parties having to agree on modifying a contract after the fact. And though most publishers would want to be fair to their authors, sometimes other external factors work against this – like falling revenue from their main income stream, physical books.

One way of dealing with risk that protects both parties is including a tiered royalty provision. Here, the content creator is guaranteed a base royalty rate of 10% no matter badly a book sells, but, if it achieves good sales, they are rewarded with a higher royalty percentage when sales reach a certain threshold. The threshold would have to vary depending on the genre. Having a threshold at 5,000 copies for poetry would certainly be pie-in-the-sky for all but TS Eliot and the Griffin Prize winners. But the tiered system certainly builds in the incentive to both parties to work hard at achieving sales, and publishers are generally more than happy to share the benefits when a title 'breaks out' of the projected sales realm.

Contract Language

Provisions covering electronic rights are certainly nothing new in the book publishing industry, but the exercise of those rights was rare until recently, except in the case of best selling titles. Publishers included these clauses just in case they were needed, not because they had any definite plans to exploit them. In fact, electronic rights seldom were exploited.

In the current climate, publishers are getting more serious about exercising electronic clauses, but the traditional wording may be too vague and general to cover what's happening on the eBook front. Content creators have a right to have details in the contract regarding the extent to which publishers plan to exploit digital channels, at what point they will issue digital versions, and the degree to which they are obliged to at least inform the content creators about what is happening or even consult them about the channels where content is to be released.

In the case of titles that are projected to have high volume sales, the publishers may be happy to cover the digital distributors' set-up and archiving costs. However, for low volume titles, the publisher may well look to the content creators to 'invest' in the costs in exchange for a higher royalty percentage, or accept a lower figure where the publisher reckons the level of sales may not warrant expending resources on conversion, etc.

I expect that creators would prefer to be given the option of 'investing' in digital versions rather than having the publisher decide that the risk is too high to cover all the costs and not do it. But this underlines the importance of looking at the wording of the digital provisions and following up on any that attach conditions to the exploitation of rights. You should ask the publisher what conditions would be minimal for the exercising of digital rights and explore cost sharing if you are keener on seeing your work in digital form than the publisher is prepared to be in writing.

Who Owns What in the Digital Version

Ownership of digital versions is another topic worth looking at. Most content creators understand that they have intellectual property rights in the ideas behind the work and how it is expressed in written form. Certainly this extends to the work's expression in digital channels.

But what about the layout and design of the work – the publisher's area of intellectual property? Elements like the design of the cover and internals are generally owned by the publisher. The exception is in the case of 'assisted' self-publication, where the creator covers the cost of the editorial, layout and design functions, and is entitled to 'own' the resulting expression of that work. Moving into the digital realm can involve the creation of multiple formats, each an entity that can be considered intellectual property.

It may well be worthwhile for creators to ask for provisions that not only gives them access to the eBook masters, but also the right to on-sell or distribute the content themselves. As we've seen, numerous digital distributors will accept content from individual content creators. So, if your publisher ends up creating the digital versions and then not properly exploiting them, you could choose to do it yourself – but only if that right is written into your contract, or excluded from it altogether.

Subsidiary rights is another area that needs to be revisited in the light of eBooks and other digital versions of work. There are conventional areas such as radio or television production that are normally covered under secondary rights provisions, but the historical description of these channels may not be flexible enough to cover emerging areas such as digital radio and TV, blogs, video sites, etc.

Film rights have traditionally been off-limits for contracts dealing with physical books, but with an increasing number of multimedia spin-offs being created for some of the new platforms like the iPad and Nook, we're seeing content moving closer and closer to the film channel – with a blurring of the distinction between what is 'film' and what is 'multimedia'. It will likely become less costly and therefore more feasible to do a cross-over from book to film, and publishers may well want to negotiate new clauses in this area.

For further information on the exciting possibilities for trans-media collaboration between publishers and multimedia companies leading to hybrid works, check out digireado's blog.

Territory Slippage

The notion of territory is probably as old as the publishing industry itself. In parallel with the days of the Empire, territories were sometimes more closely related to politics than geography.

For years, English publishers regarded Australia and New Zealand and other post-colonial countries as part of their territory, giving them easy access to these markets. It didn't work quite as well in reverse for authors from these countries, who were regarded, if at all, as second-rate by the mother country.

Old habits die hard, but the digitisation of the industry is steadily eroding the notion of territory. This is even though distributors like Amazon and Apple require publishers to identify the extent of their territorial rights before a title can be published online.

While in theory it should be possible to maintain territories in the new era, publishers will be more driven to insist on world rights in contract negotiations, to protect their revenue stream as print sales continue to slump. And if a work is pirated and then distributed by a third party – always the content creator's worst nightmare – how do you prove who has breached the territory provisions? And is there really any point in pursuing the pirates?

This only underlines the need for content creators to look closely at the scope of territories their publishers are asking for. Content creators should also ask for clauses that encourage action on the publisher's part to exploit digital opportunities within tight time limits. When these time limits expire, the scope of digital rights should be revisited or even terminated under this clause, if the publisher doesn't deliver a revenue stream that is comparable to similar books in the marketplace.

In reality, at least in the short term, it will be difficult to establish benchmarks to judge this performance. But certainly there needs to be some termination provision, to protect the content creator where the publisher does little or nothing to generate revenue from digital sales.

Most contracts already include time limits, after which rights may automatically revert to the creator if a new contract is not negotiated in place of the old one. Given the flux in the industry, creators would do well to push for shorter overall limits, such as a year. Alternatively, creators should seek at least a provision that make it possible to revisit royalty levels and subsidiary rights in all applicable contract clauses, if the publishing climate changes in the face of technological innovation – as it is at present and as it will certainly continue to do.

Epilogue: Moving Forward

The only thing that is absolutely certain in digital publishing is that uncertainty has had a chilling effect on potential partnerships between the key players: publishers, content creators, agents and distributors. Publishing was a feudal industry until recently, and the pace of change in things digital has forced publishers to leave their comfort zone to survive. Matters are not helped by the nostalgia associated with curling up with the physical book, and increasingly publishers are using this nostalgia as a rationale for inaction, rather than taking their proper measure of where the market is heading.

There are still many publishers out there eager to pull the plug on their digital programs at the first sign of market indifference. Sadly for the dinosaurs, the trends are clear and unambiguous: physical book sales are dropping, and eBook sales are increasing dramatically. In Christmas 2010, when most eBook retailers were experiencing a modest increase in sales, 45% of Australian booksellers reported a drop in physical book sales.

Up until recently, few booksellers were contemplating adding eBooks to their inventory. Many are still heading in the opposite direction, becoming increasingly cautious about ordering in even physical stock that isn't a sure winner. Some publishers are seeing the increased irrelevance of such booksellers – especially the chains – to their bottom line, and are concentrating their efforts on promoting to online stores and distributors.

Progressive booksellers should be embracing digital sales as a means of countering the drift away from physical sales. We could learn a lesson from photo shops that now do very little photo development other than top end enlargement. These shops now have self-service kiosks instead, that customer can use to develop their photos on quality printers. Bookshops could provide a similar service for downloading digital titles onto micro cards or directly onto Readers via USB or Bluetooth connection. It's early days with kiosks like Ingram's Espresso Machine, but if the demand is there, the technology will improve to meet it.

Some local booksellers like Readings in Melbourne are taking the plunge and setting up their own eBook Store linked to their existing online store. This is an important development for local industry and content creators, which will provide Australian readers with a first port of call for Australian content. However, ventures like this will only succeed if they can link seamlessly by affiliation with global players like Amazon, Kobo, Apple and Google.

The greatest challenge facing content creators and their publishers is ensuring that their work is *visible* to its audience, rather than being lost amidst the millions of new titles that will be vying for attention on the global servers. Governments have a key role to play in ensuring that cultural identity is not sacrificed on the altar of universal accessibility. There may be an argument for countries to establish national portals that can serve as a first port of call for people looking for culturally specific content.

Physical books will continue to be published and read into the foreseeable future. Certain books are better suited to physical life, such as books with high quality images-coffee table books and children's picture books. It doesn't have to be 'either or'. Physical books can spur sales of digital books into territories inaccessible to publishers. Digital books can motivate readers to purchase the physical version, just as a 3D movie theatre showing can spur viewers into purchasing a DVD or downloading the movie from an online store for repeated viewing.

While the next few years will be a nervous time for many, the progressive among us will survive and even *prosper,* but only if we give our customers what they want, rather than what we think they should have.

The marketplace wants choice.

The marketplace wants what it wants now rather than five to ten working days down the track.

Those who give the public what they want will survive. The rest may find themselves with plenty of time to replay their VHS tapes, recalling happier times.

About Dr David P Reiter

David P Reiter is an award-winning poet, writer of fiction, trans-media artist and filmmaker, and Director of IP, an innovative print and digital publisher in Brisbane, Australia.

His most recent publication is the multiplatform work *My Planets: a fictive memoir,* which is a book, an enhanced eBook, a feature-length film, and an interactive website and Facebook page. This work was completed during his latest residency at the Banff Centre for the Arts, with the support of grants from the Australia Council and the Cultural Fund of the Copyright Agency (Australia). His most recent short film, *Nullarbor Song Cycle,* was short-listed for the 2012 Western Australian Premier's Award.

His fourth book, *Hemingway in Spain and Selected Poems,* was shortlisted for the Adelaide Festival Awards. His previous books include *The Cave After Saltwater Tide* (Penguin, 1994), for which he won the Queensland Premier's Poetry Award. His book of short fiction, *Triangles,* was shortlisted for the 2000 Steele Rudd Award.

Other significant works are *The Gallery,* an interactive multimedia work completed while he was in residence at the Banff Centre for the Arts in Canada; *Kiss and Tell, Selected and New Poems* 1987-2002; and *Sharpened Knife,* a multimedia murder mystery. *The Greenhouse Effect,* a novel for junior readers, was published by Lothian Books (Hachette-Livre) in 2004, and is now being developed into an animated film. ***Global Cooling*** and ***Tiger Tames the Min Min*** are sequels in his Project Earth-mend sci-fi environmental junior novel series.

His radio play about the relationship between the painters Gauguin and Van Gogh, *Paul & Vincent,* was produced by ABC Radio National and 4MBS Classical FM, followed by the release of a version on CD.

David has been writer-in-residence at a number of places, including Bundanon (the Arthur Boyd property near Nowra), in Auckland, New Zealand at the Michael King Centre, and as Established Writer-in-Residence at the KSP Writers Centre in Perth in 2010.

He has taught at several universities in Canada and Australia and led many workshops on creative writing and publishing. Regarded as a publishing futurist, he is much in demand as a keynote speaker and presenter at festivals and conferences in Australia and abroad. David also shares his experience through a career mentorship program.

Made in United States
North Haven, CT
05 November 2026

21766928R00083